近代散佚戲曲文獻集成・名家文獻編 34

總主編 黃天驥

梅蘭芳研究海外文獻集編（下）

叢書編委會 編

山西人民出版社
三晉出版社

MEI LAN-FANG
IN
AMERICA
REVIEWS & CRITICISMS

Mei Lan-Fang

MEI LAN-FANG
IN
AMERICA

REVIEWS AND CRITICISMS

MEI LAN-FANG IN AMERICA
REVIEWS AND CRITICISMS

TABLE OF CONTENTS

CHAPTER	PAGE
I. IN PERIODICAL LITERATURE	
1. "Mei Lan-fang and His Company in Repertory" by STARK YOUNG (*The New Republic*)	3
2. "Mei Lan-fang Attracts the Most Attention" by MARY F. WATKINS (*The Dance Magazine*)	8
3. "Mei Lan-fang" by STARK YOUNG (*Theatre Arts Monthly*)	10
4. "Mei Lan-fang's New Program" by STARK YOUNG (*The New Republic*)	25
5. "Dramatic Rhythms and Mei Lan-fang" by E. V. WYATT (*Gatholic World*)	26
II. IN THE DAILY PRESS	
A. First-Night Reviews in New York	
1. *New York World:* By ROBERT LITTELL	31
2. *New York Times:* By J. BROOKS ATKINSON	32

TABLE OF CONTENTS

CHAPTER		PAGE

    3. *New York Herald-Tribune:* By ARTHUR RUHL 33
    4. *New York Evening Graphic:* By GILBERT SELDES 34
    5. *New York Evening Post:* By JOHN MASON BROWN 35
    6. *New York Morning Telegraph:* By WHITNEY BOLTON 37

B. Later Reviews in New York
    1. *New York Herald-Tribune:* By ARTHUR RUHL 39
    2. *New York World:* By WILLIAM BOLITHO . 40
    3. *A Playgoer's Notebook:* By ROBERT LITTELL 41
    4. *Albany Press:* By Gilbert Swan . . . 42
    5. *New York Times:* By JOHN MARTIN . 42
    6. *Commonweal:* By R. D. SKINNEN . . 43

C. Reviews in Other American Cities
    1. *Chicago Daily Tribune:* By GAIL BORDEN 45
    2. *Los Angles Examiner:* 46
    3. *San Francisco Chronicle:* By GEORGE C. WARREN 47
    4. *Riverside Enterprise:* 48

III. AN EVALUATION TWO YEARS LATER
"Ambassador in Art" By STARK YOUNG . . . 53
(*The New Republic, 1932*)

PREFACE

The success of Mei Lan-fang in America was as surprising as it was gratifying. Before he started on the venture, there was much doubt and trepidation as to how he and the Chinese theatrical art would be received in a foreign land. The conventions of the Chinese theatre, it was feared, might be inaccessible to Western sensibility. One good-natured pessimist predicted that Mr. Mei would be able to fill a New York theatre for three nights—and only half-full!

The New York performances began on February 16, 1930. Only two weeks were announced. The reception was so overwhelmingly favorable that by the third day after the opening, all seats for the two-week engagement were sold. It was reported that the tickets, at the box-office price of three dollars and eight-five cents, reached the high mark of eighteen dollars in the hands of the unscrupulous speculating ticket-sellers.

The engagement was extended once and again. If the company had not already promised to appear in other cities, such as Chicago and San Francisco, the "run" in New York would have lasted much longer than the five weeks Mr. Mei actually played there.

A success of such dimension could not have been due to curiosity alone. There must be something in the Chinese theatrical art and the unique accomplishments of Mei Lan-fang that artistically satisfied the American audiences. As to the nature of the Chinese theatrical art, an analysis has been made and published in "Mei Lan-fang and the Chinese Theatre." The present collection of reviews and criticisms that appeared in American journals and daily papers may serve as evidence that the acclamation was not only universal but also quite intelligently appreciative. We are especially gratified to include the articles written by the learned and distinguished critic, Stark Young. He was so kind and courteous as to remember the occasion even two years after Mr. Mei's visit.

P. C. CHANG

Tientsin
January, 1935

Fei Chen-o and the "Tiger" General

I. IN PERIODICAL LITERATURE

1. MEI LAN-FANG AND HIS COMPANY IN REPERTORY

By Stark Young

Forty-ninth Street Theater February 16, 1930

(The New Republic, March 5, 1930)

We know how much is, ordinarily, seen in the arts—very little indeed by the average eye; and how much rubbish is talked, rubbish that is somewhat insincere, faddish, imitative or else fetched up from sentiments within the speaker and not from any perception of the work of art. How much more chance, then, a review of Mr. Mei Lan-Fang has of being oblique, bluffing or fatuous! In his case more than in most, a criticism is apt to be mere autobiography on the critic's part.

In an art that belongs within the tradition of an old race, and in the presence of an artist considered by them a great artist, a good part of our attendance must be taken with humility. I spent a fair part of my time, during this performance of the Chinese company, trying merely to learn, as one learns a language. We see what we can, and must be thankful for what perception is granted us. In this performance of Mei Lan-Fang I saw enough to see that for me it was the highest point in the season's theater and in any season since Duse's visit and the Moscow Art Theater's production of Chekhov's plays.

As to the Chinese theater, we perceive in the first place that it is an art based on music, or at least musically seen, and is a complete art consisting of music, speech and dancing in the full sense, which includes dance movement, gymnastic, pantomime and gesture. Most of the music was lost on me, of course, with its foreign scale and intention, but I was surprised to find how much it takes on meaning for an outsider and how often the themes are easily distinguishable. But most of all I was struck by the mingling of music and action that I saw on the stage, the admirable accentuation of gesture by music, the way in which the music gave the tempo to the acting; and by the security of an effect achieved through such delicate means. I could tell, however foreign the music, or rather his tone, by a curious brightness and metal, that Mei Lan-Fang's voice was unusual, and that the poetic wholeness of his art arose from an astonishing unity of time, tone, emotional rhythm and bodily control.

This Chinese art is, in the second place, stiffened and syllabled with conventions; some of which are familiar to us and thought of largely with naive, indulgent humor, but many of which, not known at all, underlie like an alphabet, the entire theatrical occasion. The masks of these faces, painted with black predominating where fierceness is to be symbolized, with blue for cruelty, red for heroic, and so on; the stage properties, where moving a chair may imply another apartment, through whose imaginary door you bend to pass; the duster of horsehair, denoting the divine, the heroic, the holy; the whip standing for the horse; the usages of the sleeve; the use of the eyes, hands; the prologue on the actor's entrance, the couplet following; there are these and numberless other conventional symbols. Foreigners seize on them for harmless discussions—the easiest way out of so far-off an art. We cannot dwell upon them here, but it is interesting to consider their relation to us. There is one element to them—whether we know their implications or not—is the symbolistic. When purely symbolistic, these conventions represent—without producing—ideas, actions, things, exactly as words do, which in themselves are nothing but sound. There is this difference, however, between these symbols and words; a movement or object symbolizing a beautiful idea,

— 4 —

personage, place, tends to be created into something in itself more beautiful and worthy of the association, whereas a word remains the same, plus perhaps our effort to put beauty into its employment. These conventions in themselves have doubtless, therefore, taken on a greater and greater perfection.

It is interesting also to note the Greek and Elizabethan parallels in this Chinese theater, the obvious and slighter Elizabethan ones, mostly theater mechanics, the more profound Greek characteristics. One of these Greek similarities consists of the scenes, developed over and over again and falling into types, the Parting Scenes, Recognition Scenes, Ironic Scenes and so on. The other is the method practised always by the Greeks—a method that is based on our physical nature—we rise to song with an excess of vitality—and that has always seemed to me inevitable in the highest development of the theater—I mean the rising into music where the pitch of the dramatic idea and emotion seems to require it.

It is interesting to note the antiquity of this Chinese theater, going back almost thirty centuries perhaps, the continuity and innovations in its history, its deep relation to the Chinese soul, the innovations and inventions that are credited to Mei Lan-Fang; and to note the fact that the Chinese see these plays from time to time throughout their lives, which means listening to and learning a prefection,—something like great music heard many times, always different, always the same—which is one of the signs of excellence in any work of art, and of sophistication rather than semi-barbarism in a theater public.

Of Mei Lan-Fang himself, such facts as that he is the greatest actor in China, a public idol, with the highest honors, "The Foremost of the Pear Orchard" and the head of the Ching-Chung Monastery, that he was an accomplished musician at seven, a success in feminine roles at twelve, and that his house, collections and position in Chinese culture to-day are known over China—these things we can read in a hundred places.

Taking him—in the way an actor as a dramatic medium must be taken—as we take a musical instrument or the pigment for a painter, we see that Mei Lan-Fang is of medium height, slender, with sure, close-knit muscles, small, supple wrists, superb support in the waist—from which the fine movements and gestures of the torso proceed—a remarkable control of the neck, and perfect poise and suspension in the ankles. His face is the classic Chinese oval, with highly expressive eyes. His make-up, that overlay of carmines and darker tones, is the most beautiful I have ever seen in a theater. The diction is sharp and always pointed. The famous hands are curiously like those in Boticelli, Simone Martini and other painters of the fifteenth century. They are rather tense in form, with long fingers, squarish tipped; not so much our ideal of the hand, which is based on the sixteenth century of Reubens and Wan Dyke, but incredibly trained in the conventions and dance of the Chinese actor's art. And even with no knowledge of that art, you can see with what perfection he begins his speech, prolongs the word that gives the musicians the cue to begin, retards the words by which the music is warned to stop.

For our purposes, however, it seems to me that this is unimportant compared with one point that bears on all art basically. I mean the relation of the art of Mei Lan-Fang—the greatest in his field—to reality. That question of the relation of art to reality is the greatest of all questions with regard to art. It parallels—to employ the terms closest to us humanly—the relation of the spirit to the body, or, to invert the two terms, of the passing of the permanent, the casual in the moment to the flower of it.

On this subject much has been written about Chinese art and about this actor that is misleading. We will stick to Mei Lan-Fang. About this actor we are told to note his impersonation of women and his impersonation of various emotions. Words are weak and dependent things, and nothing could be more confusing than these are likely to be. In the first place, there is no attempt to impersonate a woman. The female roles are the most important in the Chinese theater; and he, in the kind of female role that he presents, strives only to convey the essence of the female quality, with all its grace, depth of feeling, its rhythm of tenderness and force. This distillation of the material he employs into its inherent and ideal qualities, Mei Lan-Fang does with an economy both brilliant and secure, a studious care, delicacy and inner music. The impression is one of a perfection, at once fragile and secure, that is astonishing.

But even more important—the Chinese critics have already often warned us about the female roles—even more important for us is the matter of his realism in general. I found myself most impressed in this regard during the piece from the Ming Dynasty, where the princess stabs the general who has destroyed her family, and then kills herself with his sword. This seemed to me more satisfying than the play about the husband's return, for in the last it was easy to see the movement away from the older, high style. What we must say about the realism and abstraction and stylization of Mei Lan-Fang's art is that, exactly as in the case in the classic Chinese art, we are astonished at the precision of its realistic notations and renderings, and are dazzled by the place these take in the highly stylized and removed whole that the world of art becomes. These movements of Mei Lan-Fang, that way he has of keeping the whole body alive, even in the stillest moments of the action, of putting that continuous movement or vibration into the head as it springs from the neck; that voice that in its sheer tone moves away from actuality; that sophisticated, poetic use of the eyes, those expressions of fear, pity, murderous resolution, despair, and so on, that come over his face; none of these is impersonation or reality in the usual sense. They are real only in the sense that great sculptures or paintings are real, through their motion in repose; their impression of shock, brief duration and beautiful finality. Every now and then—very rarely—in acting we see this happen: I mean a final creation, free from merely incidental matter, of an essential quality in some emotion, the presentation of that truth which confirms and enlarges our sense of reality. But I have never seen it so securely and repeatedly achieved as in Mei Lan-Fang.

* * * * *

2. MEI LAN-FANG ATTRACTS THE MOST ATTENTION

(*The Dance Magazine, May, 1930*)

By Mary F. Watkins

Volumes could, and in fact should, be written upon the art and personality of this young man who, although still in his early thirties, is the leading actor-dancer in all of China, the idol of five hundred million people. It is, however, more properly the meat of the dramatic reviewer, for superlative as is Mr. Mei's dancing, he is primarily of the complete theater. We will not, therefore, dilate in these columns upon the ancient and delicate art which, although frankly outside the experience and comprehension of Western audiences, contains within its stylized formalism and tradition a grace, clarity and persuasion which can not be comprised or even approached on our more naturalistic, cruder Occidental stage. We will speak only of the two numbers on this first program which come within the scope of the dance reviewer, the *Duel Scene from the Green Stone Mountain*, and the sword dance contained within the episode of the *King's Parting with his Favorite*.

The first of these was performed by a member of the Company who took the part of the Fox-in-the-body-of-a-beautiful-woman. In this conventional simulation of a duel the art of juggling is carried to superlative virtuosity, and the young man's manipulation of two tasselled wands actually electrified the audience. The dance began, however, with a formalized rhythmic movement for two actors with spears, and gradually developed, after much of the actual fighting had seemed to be accomplished, into a whirlwind of flashing, twirling sticks, a series of balancing feats which defied the quickness of the human eye. The dance terminated with a succession of spectacular falls which would bring blushes to the cheek of the most talented tumblers on any vaudeville circuit in the Western hemisphere. Nothing like it had ever been seen by at least one fairly experienced reporter, and the performance left the audience actually more breathless than the actor, who took his recalls in the customary calm and unruffled Oriental manner.

Mr. Mei's own dance occurred at the end of the bill, and we understand that since the first performance, the dramatic and spoken part of the incident has been shorn away, and thus left the field free for this dance which lasts without interruption for some eight minutes. It is a *tour de force* of adroitness, skill and grace, tied up in form and symbolism, but in no sense impeded by them.

We have no less an authority than Mr. Shawn (who met Mei Lan-Fang in China and studied his art by means of special performances very graciously accorded), for the fact that this actor is entirely responsible for the introduction of these dance episodes into the ancient form of the Chinese drama, and that a great deal of opposition met this innovation among the fundamentalists of his native land. That he has been eminently successful, however, is proved by his position to-day, and by the fact that in the repertoire which he brings to this country under the auspices of the China

Institute in America, there are eleven different dances and ballets included, of which we shall hope, before his engagement terminates, to see the greater part.

* * * * *

3. MEI LAN-FANG

BY STARK YOUNG

(Theatre Arts Monthly, Vol. 14, April, 1930)

The conventions of the Chinese theatre are more or less known to many foreigners, and if not, can be easily read about. One way or another, such conventions as stooping, to show that you pass through a door, the property men who are to move things about and to be regarded meanwhile as themselves invisible, the whip to represent a horse, are fairly common knowledge. There are numberless others, from such simple representations as the duster of horsehair that denotes divine or eminent persons, or walking on the knees to denote trembling with fear, to the more elaborate conventions in the dancing, the music and musical instruments, the usage of the sleeves, the diverse modes for entrances and exits, the costumes, the masks of the faces, painted—by formulas, for the most part ancient—with a predominant red to signify the heroic, with blue for cruelty, and so on. These conventions are sometimes distant and elusive; in their simpler forms they are innocently smiled at among foreigners, in much the same way as the tilt of the head and arrangement of the limbs in Byzantine painting or in Botticelli or the archaic smile and eyes of early Greek sculpture, are smiled at; and are naively taken to imply that the artist did not know how things actually look and had stumbled but blindly toward the light. It is of course easier to dwell thus on any departure from reality than it is to learn the alphabet of an art and to read its language. But to dwell very much on these conventions in Mei Lan-fang's art is a mistake.

An account of Mei Lan-fan's life and work is as readily found as an account of the Chinese theatre. He was a musician at seven, a successful player of female roles at twelve; he is the greatest Chinese actor, is "Foremost of the Pear Orchard" and head of the Ching-Chung Monastery, the highest titles in his art. He has a repertory of four hundred plays. He has made profound studies into the arts of China, has revived many old forms in plays, music and dancing, and through his tact and genius combined these with his country's modern theatrical art; for example, the old classical dances of China, which he has set to the music of to-day. He has combined styles hitherto strictly separate in Chinese tradition—the operatic and histrionic female roles, for example—and from either of them has drawn at will, in order from such a fusion to enrich and increase the flexibility of his portrayal. He has created a school or tradition that involves every element in the theatre, costume, music, realism, stylization, spoken and sung speeches, and so on. As a medium for the art of acting we may record that, however foreign his music may be, his voice is plainly one of great flexibility, brightness and dramatic timbre; his muscular control, based on dancing and acrobatics, is remarkable; his mask mobile, accurate and trained to that passive and exact restraint that we see in good Chinese sculpture; his eyes somewhat larger than those of most Chinese and highly expressive; his famous hands slender and trained to the utmost in the conventional and complex uses of his art. He is medium height; the face oval; the waist, from which so much of his gesture and movement pivot, is supple, well-knit and thoroughly disciplined. The nervous co-ördination is so manifestly responsive to the action around him on the stage, and so almost supernaturally sensitive to the audience, that it becomes one of the chief sources of his magnetism, and might indeed become, if he should play too long for foreign audiences, a source of danger to the purity and wholeness of his art.

This Chinese theatre brought to us by Mei Lan-fang is not necessarily the greatest kind of theatre art; we should only waste time getting into that discussion. What counts for us just now, and makes the event of so much point, is that, far beyond anything in the Western theatre, it is a theatre that is pure and that is complete. Saying that it is pure art does not mean that, like music or architecture, it exists solely within its own terms, entirely without reference to anything outside itself, for no theatre could be without some degree of verisimilitude. This Chinese theatre, like any other, is constantly based on resemblance, on a truth to the life we see among men and to the world that we look upon or dream of. Even its conventions are largely stylizations of actual conditions of place or action. This is the point and is a matter that must be put carefully: the purity of this Chinese theatre art consists in the fact that everything employed in it—action, facial expression, voice, movement, speech, the story, the place and so on—is so subordinated to the artistic intention that the resulting work is in itself an entity wholly ideal, a work of art, at no point to be mistaken for actuality. To say that this Chinese art is not necessarily inclusive of all human experience but is as theatre art complete, means that it draws on every medium of this particular art, acting, speech, singing, music, dancing in the wide meaning of the term, visual décor and, finally, the audience, for the players include the audience in their technique as definitely and frankly as any other element. Furthermore, this is a theatre with an exact and passionately left tradition behind it, a severe discipline and apprenticeship and an exacting public, so that whatever, good or bad, is done, can be taken as settled and intentional and ready to be judged. And it is based on great sophistication, for the audience, with

— 12 —

the story and characters already known, and all merely incidental realism dispensed with, is concerned with the performance itself, its quality and progress. Mei Lan-fang's theatre, then, is a veritable school of principles for us to consider.

We watch *The Death of the Tiger General.* It is a play from the Ming Dynasty, a sixteenth century piece. I take it because it is the most complete and admirable number on Mei Lan-fang's present program, less flexible, free or intimate than the play about the slipper; and more austere, fixed and in the grand style. The walls, a permanent set, painted to represent open brick work or lacquer, with two doors, left and right, at the back, are hung with embroidered tapestries. Fei Chen-o, a court lady, has taken the place of the imperial princess, who has promised to wed the Tiger General in order more securely to kill him and avenge her family, whose ruin he has worked. She enters, sings an aria in which she sets forth her intention, and in this and her soliloquy and dance, expresses her varying states of mind, the vengeance, shame, horror, resolution, seduction and murder. The Tiger General enters, somewhat overcome by the wine with which his fellow officers have toasted him in honor of his betrothal. Fei Chen-o beguiles him into drinking more wine, the nuptial couch is brought in by the property men, the General takes off his helmet and coat and falls asleep. Fei Chen-o calls her maids to make her ready. They remove her head-dress, her belt studded with jade, and her magnificent coat. She sends the attendants away, looks behind the curtain to see if the Tiger General is asleep, plunges her dagger into his breast. A struggle follows in which an old wound is struck, he falls, she kills him with his own sword, which she snatches from where it hangs above the couch. Then follows a song of her dread of the soldiers, of shame, of death; she cuts her throat with the sword and falls lifeless.

I am shaken with an excitement that is curiously stronger than I am likely to get from any mere photographic portrayal of death and horror and is yet at the same time vaguer and more exalted; and then gradually the points that are important to me, and greatly so to our Western theatre, begin to range themselves in my mind.

I hear the music of the orchestra, the ti-tzu, or flute, once used in the older aristocratic theatre and reinstated in Chinese favour through Mei Lan-fang's influence, the cymbal, flutes and other instruments. The scale is foreign to our ears but much of the music becomes easily distinguishable and dramatic in effect. I see that this Chinese theatre art is based on music, or at least musically seen, it is felt as moving continuously within the realm of music. I note the fine accentuation of the gesture by music, the tapping of a drum, or, in this classic drama especially, the noble line of the flute, without the quarter notes, without the trills that some of the musical modes allow, but grave, austere, leading on the tragic emotion. Sometimes the emotional content of the scene opens more fully and follows the musical idea given to it by the orchestra. I realize more than ever that the final quality, pure and ideal, of a work of theatre art is measured by the degree of its motion toward music, the sense, whether the music be heard or only felt continuously, of resting on musical life.

I note the rising into song whenever the pitch of the emotion seems to demand it, which is biologically true—since with an access of vitality it is natural for us to burst into song— and which seems to me a natural and necessary condition in the highest development of the theatre art. The Greeks practiced it; the Church has always known how to preserve, in the drama of the mass, this alternation of spoken and sung levels of feeling; and Shakespeare and Marlowe, in the absence of such a technical possibility, did what they could to make up for the lack by an extreme heightening of the style, straining their poetic medium to its last mad divinity.

I note in this Chinese theatre that of the medium involved that of the actor is quite frankly the chief; which is sound doctrine since he, of all these mediums, has most connection with the audience, who are human beings like himself.

I notice at once that Mei Lan-fang's make-up is the most beautiful I have ever seen, those various carmines that shade his eyes and give them the contours of the eyes in classic Chinese sculpture, that black of the eyebrows underlaid with red, and blended into the surrounding white, like painted porcelains, that sharp outline of the hair arranged about the face in order to define the type desired. The face of the Tiger General is painted into a complete mask, black, white, red, in flat patterns.

I notice in Mei Lan-fang's acting that the rhythms of the body are complete throughout. If a gesture is made with the right hand, it not only proceeds from the right shoulder (in much of the acting we see hereabouts not even that occurs) but affects the left shoulder as well; so that the entire torso falls into the justly related rhythms. The head is constantly moving, subtly alive on the neck, a motion that may often be unnoticed, as we may overlook the vibration of line and plane in fine sculpture. The use of the sleeves, from which hang the long white cuffs far down below the hands, is, in Mei Lan-fang, regarded by his Chinese public as the height of all his accomplishments. The variety of these usages and conventions a foreigner could only observe after a long familiarity with his art, but the beauty and drama of the dance that he creates from them is evident. At one moment in the play, after Fei Chen-o has put off her head-dress and coat, and stands dressed in her blue jacket with its white linings and white sleeves and the long dress of white, she flees in terror from the maddened Tiger General, and you see the sleeves go up, wildly fluttered, like a white dove, you even hear the flutter of wings in quick flight; a thing so subtly done and perfect that you can hardly believe it happened, and yet it was done with great certainty and design, even to its exact position on the stage.

I note the acrobatic display in this Chinese acting, softened or stiffened according to the character. Of this fact we may say that, for one thing it is based on a fundamental muscular impulse within our bodies; and, for another, that this acrobatic technique serves to relate the actor, through the medium of his body, more fluently and more accurately, to the musical basis on which his art relies.

Of the many conventions and symbols, I note how, even those that are as symbolic as a word—which, of course, means nothing until you learn what it represents—have tended, because of their significance and association, to acquire a degree of perfection in themselves—the stooping to enter a door, for example, the hiding of the face during emotion at certain times, the symbolic objects themselves, those decorative whips, dusters, parts of the costume. I note the precision where precision is desired for the whole effect—a movement of blowing out the light is as exact as the most realistic actor of great talent could make it.

My mind experiencing all this is filled with the various imports. The first of these concerns realism in art. This is, after all, the greatest question in art, and parallels what is the greatest question in our life: the relation of the actual around us to ourselves, of our own bodies to our minds and souls, of what is permanent in time to what is passing, the extent to which the world is related to us and restated within us for our own uses, the necessity we feel for singing the world of our experience with the name of our dreams. This Chinese theatre is spoken of as completely unrealistic art, entirely ideal in character. But while this is in a larger sense true, we must be careful not to be misled. This theatre art of Mei Lan-fang is not completely without realism, not in the sense that a cubistic painting would be, an abstract Arabic decoration, a geometric dance design. Its exact parallel is Chinese painting and sculpture. In these the impression that remains in the memory is of the abstract and decorative, but we are constantly surprised at the exactitude with which nature, a leaf, a bough, a bird, a hand, a mantle, has been observed, and are amazed at the dazzling notation of characteristic details and at the manner in which they are made to supercede and concentrate their own actuality. This exact notation is marvellously set into the whole work of art, which taken in its completeness, is ideal and dreamlike. To judge even by their common paintings and statuettes, the delight felt by the Chinese in this dexterous realism combined with tradition, convention and abstract pattern, must be very strong. We are to remember this when we hear it said that Mei Lan-fang's art is wholly unrealistic. We must also remember that one of the things to learn from this Chinese theatre art is not the need for unrealism or its contrary, but rather the exactness of the degree to which, in every part of it, realism is employed. The gestures, the narration, the acting, even the much discussed falsetto voice employed for the female roles, the movement, and so on, all are the same distance from the actual; which is another way of saying that the whole achieves a total unity of style.

But there is a reverse observation about this art that is also misleading. With the matter of the commonly heard phrase, the female impersonator, we need not concern ourselves. The Chinese themselves have often warned us, and we have only to use our senses, to see that Mei Lan-fang does not attempt to represent a woman. He seeks to discover and recreate certain essential qualities in movement, emotional rhythm, grace, force of will, seduction, vivacity or tenderness; and from these to present a figure, secure in its feminine attributes and persuasion, created into the pattern of a dance, poetic in essence. But in the matter of those impersonations of emotion and states of mine of which we hear so much—of fear, hate, love et cetera—we must get the point straight. There is no intention of acting out an emotion or of portraying the actual expression that would accompany such an emotion in life. The intention, again, is that which we see in good Chinese statues and paintings. The motion is stilled into something less immediate than the actual emotion in life; it contrives to give us the shock of truth without the incidental intrusion of imitation or photography; we have the sense of action in repose, of finalities within a flux of forms, or something beautiful and elusive. Words can scarcely express this point, but, from the realm of our own culture, we have, in order to realize it, only to look at some work of Mino da Fiesole, Desiderio da Settignano, Rosellino, for exapmle, or Duccio, noting the flow of the essential lines, the concentration toward some ideal harmony, the sense of some beautiful transcription of reality and that elusive flight from it to the permanent.

This idealistic flexibility, with regard to the use of the actual, leads the Chinese theatre art into the freedom of our profoundest human truth, into purities of rendering essential quality, and into confirmations of the human mind, not as dependent for its proofs on things outside itself, but as a reality among other realities. In that last scene of the play where Fei Chen-o grovels with her despair, draws the sword across her throat, and falls, crumpled and motionless, down the floor—that stillness, which is like the stillness and sudden darkness that must come suddenly thus into that anguished soul—is more exact than any blood or final convulsions could be. The mingling freely of supernatural beings and mortal men, which we see constantly in these plays as a mere matter of course, is a simple rendering of one of our commonest feelings; I mean the gods, memory, the great dead, dreams, the ghosts of love, these presences that are so often within us, even beside us they seem, so real are they. There are some inner realities of which all outward evidence is only a weak obstruction to their full intensity; there is no outer reality in action or expression that would not obstruct the full effect; and here if necessary, this Chinese method permits of no reality whatever; the face, for instance, at some terrible moment is hidden with the sleeves, leaving the grief suddenly hidden from us, as, even in life, another's grief at its greatest depths must be, no matter what outward signs of it occur. Such instances as these are only a few among the many advantages of such flexibility as the Chinese theatre enjoys. As a matter of fact, to come to the point, Mei Lan-fang is freer from the bonds of these conventional traditions in his art than our theatre is from its realism; for, wishing to work a certain shock and check, whenever he likes he can successfully insert a certain amount of realistic detail, whereas one of our actors, no matter what removal and style he may long for in some passage dear to him, is tied to such gestures, manners and actual possibilities as are conceivable in life.

I have seen various survivals from other epochs—at the Theâtre Français, for instance, but never before this Chinese theater of Mei Lan-fang's have I seen a high, contemporaneous instance of the classical minded in the theatre arts. By classical in this sense I do not mean any reference to Greece and Rome necessarily but to a state of mind, an attitude in art, that on the whole accepts certain forms, certain type ideas, characters, working patterns, and takes for granted that it is within these that the artist is to express himself. In this sense Beethoven, using the strict musical forms and altering, refuting and enriching them with his own romantic soul, was not classical; nor was Michelangelo, whose magnificent and sometimes perverse treatments, in the Campidoglio, for instance, are so full of a secret and personal violence. Racine, the ancient Noh plays of Japan, the suclpture of Phidias, the mass ritual of the Catholic Church are classical minded. With regard to Mei Lan-fang's theatre it is just at this point, that one of the gravest misconceptions has arisen. We are told that in it there is a fixed way to do everything, unalterable conventions and rules, and that the secret of its beautiful persuasion lies in the fact that it is not original, not disturbed with egotism and individualism, but is all set, established, approved of by tradition, perfected by the centuries. As a matter of fact, though this is not an uncommon way of speaking of the classical, to say so is only to describe an art that is dead. When such an imprisonment within form exists, there is no art but mostly only husks, dry husks unable to contain the living content that waits to be expressed. No, the essence of the classical mind is that within this form and typicality you do not evade or nullify yourself but express yourself. Fixed though a pattern may tend to be, the creative impulse, working on it, finds itself; as many diverse men may find themselves or may express themselves, looking on the sea, which remains in its character nevertheless, or at the wide sky, in which each one creates an image. There are people who understand, and those who do not, that a prayer repeated through a thousand years by millions of lips may still contain the essence of fresh needs, just as the human body, always the same, always different, still carries the inexhaustible variety of countless souls. This classical mindedness in art, however, is not, of course, the only kind of mind, and not necessarily the most admirable. With time and movement the largest patterns and forms are due to change. The point merely is that in the Chinese theatre so far, for reasons deep within the soul and history of the race, this change has not been convulsive or obliterative: the classical mind remains.

As a matter of fact, however, Mei Lan-fang's art is by no means so fixed as all this might imply. He has not only forced traditional forms to express his own poetry and energy and wonder, but has originated many treatments, revived and illuminated many lost features of the Chinese theatre,

— 20 —

presenting them singly or in a creative fusion with contemporary forms. His performances are alive with their individual immediacy, never dry or academic. Like everything that is art instead of being merely mechanical, they press constantly against the pattern, at the same time staying within it, and by that very pressure and conformity they keep themselves alive; an exact parallel of what happens elsewhere: in life a man's individual self struggles against the human type in which he exists, remaining at the same time, unless he be a freak, within the type; in art a pattern made by hand differs from one made by machinery by this same living combination of assertion and restriction. On the whole, nevertheless, this Chinese theatre is classical; the forms remain like great aspects of the natural world, which a man accepts, and the image of which within himself he bends to his own uses.

Not only upon this quality of the classical, which may occur in any country, but also on the Greek, Mei Lan-fang's theatre is a luminous comment. The Elizabethan parallels with the Chinese theatre are obvious and more or less external. There is the fixed scene, with certain properties and conventions, naive or not naive, according as you may happen to see it; there is a bush for a forest at the Globe, a whip for a horse at the Pekin theatre, there are the four men to stand for an army, certain arbitrary positions on the stage to indicate various places, and so on. There is the prologue. There are couplets said at the Chinese actor's entrance and others said at his exit, very much as the end of the scene was often indicated in Shakespeare by a couplet:

    The time is out of joint: O cursed spite,
    That ever I was born to set it right!

There are the men playing female roles. There is the possibility of shifting back and forth between prose and verse, and of writing the play in any number of scenes.

But the comment of Mei Lan-fang's theatre on the Greek is the most profound that I have ever seen. I have seen German and English revivals of Greek dramas, done often with ingenuity, spaciousness and, at certain intervals, even with power. But the Greek element in these was only in retrospect, too self-conscious, often too theoretical, though now and then out of its own secure universality quite compelling and convincing, whether there was an authentic slant or not to the interpretation afforded us. I have seen Italian productions of Euripides and of *Oedipus Rex*, careless but not without vitality and eloquence, superbly aired beneath the sky and amidst the ruins of classic Rome; given too with some feeling of the hail and farewell that time has only increased in these tragic poems. But in none of these was the Greek element inherent and not the result of studious interest, however much we felt its poetry and beauty. I have seen numerous pieces from the classic French period, *Polyeucte*, for example, *Andromache*, with their classicistic set, and courtly version of the Greek spirit; and I saw once Mounet Sully do his Oedipus. This last, by virtue of three hundred years of tradition in the French classic theatre, had an inherent spirit, very elegant and august and often magnificently moving. And, through this authentic French tradition, plus the force of Sophocles' genius and the Greek character of the powerful story, a considerable degree of Greek quality seemed genuinely implicit in it, though a very late Greek quality, long after Athens was a mere eclectic centre of art. But this Chinese theatre is a profound comment because the qualities reminiscent of Greece represent for China a natural way of thought, a spirit deeply inherent. There are not only the patent resemblances like the men in female roles, the Chinese faces often painted into masks, with traditional styles and conventional meanings, scarely to be distinguished from the actual masking in Attic theatres, the limitation in settings, there are also resemblances in qualities that proceed from the inmost characteristics of mind and spirit. There are the fixed patterns for exits and entrances and stage movement, there is the use of the dancing medium, in the fullest sense of the term, the basis of musical accompaniment, musical accentuation, the rising into music where the emotion demands the very fullest expression, there is the fusion of words, speech, singing, music, dancing and décor into one art. There are the standard scenes, built on familiar patterns, set scenes as it were, which, as with many of our musical forms, are to be enjoyed and admired for the treatment afforded them—Recognition Scenes, Parting Scenes, Scenes Based on Irony, Dialectic Scenes and so on. There is the search for pattern, and the subordination of personal emotion to some passionate abstraction and secure outline. There is the unceasing stylization throughout. There is the intention of beauty, grace or exaltation.

It must be said, however, that there was a boldness or shock in the Greek sometimes that would be excessive for the Chinese. In *Oedipus Rex*, for example, the king, after digging out his eyes, enters with his bleeding face and his speech that begins with the pain and the physical detail of his voice seeming so far away, and moves on to the thought of that horror awaiting him in the world of the dead. In this scene the physical detail is used to clinch the impression on the audience' mind, to send the moment into their bloods and make them believe it; and the poetic details are used to create the ideal significance that lies in the moment, and to give it wings. There is nothing like that in Chinese, not in its authentic theatre. The reluctance on its part to present such physical extremes, has to doubt something to do with the racial soul, in which death and horror have their due place but are seen in a long avenue of centuries and patient thought. When Fei Chen-o approaches the Tiger General's couch, she has drawn a strand of her hair across her mouth, on which her teeth are clenched—even the abysm of hate must be covered like that or in some way prevented from ugliness, it must ultimately be beautiful.

This brings us to a final point on which there is much misconception and mistaken writing with regard to Mei Lan-fang's theater. It is often said that the sole end of this Chinese art is to achieve grace and beauty. This is entirely confusing, though, it must be confessed, to such persons and races as may have a smaller sense of beauty and grace, it is something of an easy way out.

To say that we seek grace and beauty in themselves is as foolish as to speak of seeking freedom for its own sake: we seek freedom only in order to be the better able to achieve something that we desire and aim at. We must go farther back now and start again. Then we shall say that what this Chinese art seeks primarily is the lack of what we may call effortism. That means that you have not achieved your end when you have merely arrived at an execution of what there was to do, however excellently and skillfully your effort came off. What you strive for is something that follows on this expert and complete accomplishment; I mean that when all else is accomplished, there remains the direction to be finally taken; that when all else is done, there remains to be achieved the flower, the fragrance, the soul, the last grace of it. Hence the attempt to present to us that quality of the beauty, discovery and permanence of patterns. These patterns denote and contain the soul of us. Watching Mei Lan-fang through one of his tragic scenes, I am absorbed with the thought of how this persistent weaving of life among its own beautiful forms binds and delights us. But even this grace or soul or beauty—whatever name we want to call it by—does not remain left to itself like that. It constitutes a sort of continuum, a something by which is provided the continuity that runs through one action to another, through phrase to phrase, idea to idea, and so on through all the successive parts of the play, establishing thus for it a

— 24 —

kind of music or free essence in which it moves.   We may say, moreover, looking at the drama as a social element, that it may be this final quality of grace and beauty that has given the whole Chinese theatre a freedom from which derives, more than from anything else, its continuity and endurance within the race, as if it were not only an art but a quality of soul.

* * * * *

4. MEI LAN-FANG'S NEW PROGRAM
By Stark Young

(The New Republic, Vol. 62, March, 1930)

Mei Lan-fang's new program presents first the play of the favorite who comes to the palace only to find that her lord is absent with another woman. The eunuchs try to ease her mind with assurances of his speedy return; they give her wine; she and her maids kneel to await him. The attendants are obliged at last to disillusion her; they try to mend matters by coaxing her to drink more and more. She leaves in despair.

After that there comes a play in which ridicule is used to defeat an enemy. Then comes a dance, by Mei Lan-fang and a sort of shadow partner; then a play in which a fisherman and his daughter are persecuted by an official in order to extract from them a remarkable pearl that is in their possession. The fisherman at length returns from the court bruised and beaten; he and his daughter, who is as good a fighter as he, set off, after bidding the home farewell, to kill the ruler. They are admitted to his presence under the pretext of the daughter's showing him the pearl. She cuts his throat with a sword that has been hidden beneath her cloak. She and her father then defend themselves against the guards and make their escape.

The ridicule play, in which Mei Lan-fang himself took no part, was humorous, exact and achieved with a final delightful completeness and summation, like one of the old Chinese paintings of the more burly sort. Mei Lan-fang in his numbers repeated the poetry and technical perfection that he has already shown. The movements are fluent but accurate, the effect calculated at every turn. There were the same final grace and taste, the same distillation of the material into an art. The rhythms of this art arise from a fusion of all the mediums of the theater—music, song, speech, written words, dancing. This dancing is a part of the whole. In the fisherman piece, I must add, the costumes are as beautiful as I have ever seen.

* * * * *

5. DRAMATIC RHYTHMS AND MEI LAN-FANG

By E. V. Wyatt

(Catholic world, Vol. 131, April, 1930)

Mei Lan-Fang, "Foremost of the Pear Orchard" and Abbot of Ching-chung Monastery, is the toast of the town. His art, graceful and persuasive, aloof and complex, exerts, despite the foreign falsetto of his speech and the incongruities of Chinese harmony, a lingering and compelling charm. So perfect in detail is the performance of his troupe that perhaps one does not at first appreciate that the plays have as definite a rhythm as the dances. The two short plays that are offered are dramatic trifles, neither subtle nor important. They were evidently chosen as sufficiently obvious in their content to be intelligible in pantomime. One can understand how *Hamlet* in English might suffer in Peking. What lends so much interest to the plays, apart from the acting, is their proof that in the Chinese Theatre, the drama has never been divorced from the dance. Indeed, Miss Soo Yong, whose excellent English has so impressed her audiences, explains before the curtain that every Chinese actor must be a dancer as well. The fact is evident in their every gesture and particularly implicit in the work of Mei Lan-fang whose feminine impersonations are so much enhanced by the musical quality of his movements.

The measure of those high pitched stage voices and the insistent beat of the hidden orchestra of strange instruments rings in one's ears as one leaves the theater. Just so do Shakespeare's pentameters reecho from an empty stage.

Some of our readers may remember that in January we described *Totenmal (The Call on the Dead)*, the experiment in a new form of the dramatic art that is to be given in Munich this summer. In this Herr Talhoff has used his words as an accompaniment to his dances. After studying the art of Mei Lan-fang, we were particularly interested in the letter from Mary Wigman, the chief dancer in Totenmal, whose ideas were quoted in the New York Herald Tribune of March 2nd. She Writes:

"The problem of the relation between music and the dance may be regarded as solved. But the connection of the spoken word and the dance is still an open question with unlimited possibilities. In recent years I have been repeatedly approached with the request to try to unite the dance with drama and poetry but it was only when I got to know Albert Talhoff's work that my scruples were overcome."

There are many moments on the stage when words alone are entirely inadequate. A great actor can convey with one gesture what it might take many lines to express. We very much doubt if anything that Mei Lan-fang has to say explains the infinite disgust of his delicate Ming Princess for the tawdry details of assassination and suicide which is inherent in his eyes and in the movement of his sensitive hands. It is entirely the accord of the acting to the rhythm of the music that raises this little Grand Guignol thriller to a higher place of art. In a lesser degree, Reinhardt's productions attained the same result. The rhythm of the "Marseillaise," with Tilly Losch leading the mobs, was sustained throughout Danton's *Tod*. The memory of the *Midsummer Night's Dream* is one of continuous weaving movement between mortals and fairies in pursuit of airy fancies and illusive loves. The great success of *Broadway* we have always felt was due to Jed Harris's having caught and played it in a steady rhythm of jazz. Our actors, unlike the Germans and Chinese, are unfortunately not trained in the higher forms of dance.

"The dancer of to-day," continues Mary Wigman, "keeps turning to the theater, and yet the modern theater only uses him as a virtuoso in his own art or as an interpreter of secondary musical ideas. It is not only my needs as a dancer that induce me to cooperate in *Totenmal* but I regard it as a duty which an entire generation of younger dancers has the right to expect of me as their leader."

When Miss Wigman goes on to say that "a dancer must remain in his own world of presentiment and allusion—of psychic vibration—in a word, an irrational world which may be described by words but can never be replaced by them," we are not quite sure that we follow her. But we do feel our stage is on the eve of a new and exciting development foreshadowed in the wisdom of the East, and that there is much worth our study in the fine art of Mei Lan-fang.

*   *   *   *   *

II. IN THE DAILY PRESS

The Suspected Slipper

A. FIRST-NIGHT REVIEWS IN NEW YORK

1. BY ROBERT LITTELL

(New York World, February 17, 1930)

Last night's introduction of Mei Lan-Fang, China's most famous actor, to American audiences, was one of the strangest and most exciting evenings I ever spent in a theater. I understood, perhaps, five per cent of what was going on—and misunderstood most of that—but it was enough to make me feel very humble about our stage and the Western stage in general. For here is an art so ancient, so formal, and, in its baffling tantalizing way, so perfect that what we do seems by comparison to have no tradition and no roots in the past at all.

Mei Lan-Fang and his company are here for only a few weeks. Do not fail to see him. You will understand no more than I did. You will be puzzled all the way through, and a little bored once in a while; but in spite of knowing nothing of a dramatic background that goes back to 200 or more B.C., in spite of hundreds of rigid conventions of staging and gesture, in spite of emotional values entirely different from your own, in spite of the musical accompaniment that often outrages your ears, you will be charmed and fascinated and now and then swept quite off your feet.

No matter how much you are bewildered and flounder around without any familiar dramatic furniture to take hold of, you will admit, after he has been on the stage three minutes that Mei Lan-Fang is one of the most extraordinary actors you have ever seen. An actor, singer and dancer combined, and combined so that you never see the boundary between these three arts, which as a matter of fact in the Chinese theatre are indissolubly one.

When you see him on the stage you find yourself in some timeless region as lovely and harmonious as an old fairy story. You forget that he is a man playing women's parts, according to immemorial custom, in a curious but irresistible falsetto voice. You forget everything but the picture he is making, as strong and delicate in every eloquent gesture as an old Chinese painting, very beautiful to look at for the costumes and poses alone, but also full of immensely subtle dignity and repose. And then think of our own surface, improvised acting, born yesterday and old stuff to-morrow.

Mei Lan-Fang is supported by a cast and appears in plays as to the merits of which, from a Chinese point of view, I can say less than nothing. Some of them were fascinatingly incomprehensible; others, in particular the first, wherein a husband, after a long absence, discoveres a strange slipper in his wife's room and accuses her of having a lover, were surprisingly easy to catch the drift of. Especially in the humourous moments, which Mei Lan-Fang's pantomime and changes of expression made clear to us.

These Chinese plays, and the wonderful gestures, sometimes dancing acrobats, in them, can be seen, just for the sake of the gestures they make, without understanding what they are about. They cannot be described, at least so soon after the first gulp of astonishment and joy.

Nothing like this has ever been seen in New York.

* * * * *

2. BY J. BROOKS ATKINSON

(New York Times, February 17, 1930)

Nothing an untutored Occidental can say about the art of Mei Lan-Fang, which was revealed at the Forty-ninth

Street Theatre last evening, will be of much importance except as guileless appreciation. For the drama of Peking, whence Mr. Mei and his actors come, has almost no point of similarity to the drama with which we are familiar; and the barrier of language is as nothing by comparison with the barrier of a completely exotic art. It is styled, conventionalized and as old as the hills. But it is as beautiful as an old Chinese vase or tapestry. If you can purge yourself of the sophomoric illusion that it is funny, merely because it is different, you can begin to appreciate something of exquisite loveliness in pantomime and costume, and you may feel yourself vaguely in contact, not with the sensation of the moment, but with the strange ripeness of centuries. Perhaps you may even have a few bitter moments of reflecting that although our own theatrical form is enormously vivid it is rigid, and never lives so freely in terms of imagination as this one does.

3. BY ARTHUR RUHL

(*New York Herald-Tribune, February 17, 1930*)

The noteworthy thing was the extraordinary grace and fineness which Mr. Mei brought to his impersonations—an art as perfect as it is exotic, and quite eloquent enough to charm and hold an American audience throughout the evening, even though they could but guess, most of the time, just what was being said and indicated.

To speak with any authority of Mr. Mei's technique is beyond the capacity of this spectator. Suffice to say that he is intensely interesting, throws about everything he does a curious and exotic charm, and that one feels throughout the evening, and in the work of all concerned, the presence of an ancient culture in which formalism has gone so far that the significant thing is not so much what is seen on the surface as the underlying emotion that all these conventionalized poses and gestures suggest. How far the general public will relish the performance remains to be seen, but it is something that all who take an intelligent amateur's interest in an unfamiliar art will find it worth while seeing.

* * * * *

4. BY GILBERT SELDES

(*New York Evening Graphic, February 17, 1930*)

There are two ways of looking at the Chinese plays now offered at the 49th Street Theatre; as the revelation of one of the most delicate and complicated arts of the Orient and as sheer entertainment.

I have seen a few hours of a Chinese play near Chatham Square and read some of *the Dream of the Red Chamber* and conned my program notes, but I feel far from authoritative about the art of the Chinese Theatre.

Yet what anyone can see is the extraordinary physical equipment of this actor, his absolute mastery and control of all his body, his remarkably sensitive eyes and hands, his complete characterizations, his staying always inside his characters. Foreign as everything seemed, one thing was foreign because it isn't often met with at home: a sort of artistic decorum. Little as you knew of his play or his playing, you felt that Mr. Mei was never playing down, was never making an improper appeal or deserting the high standard he had set for himself.

5. BY JOHN MASON BROWN

(New York Evening Post, February 17, 1930)

Indeed, so different from the realistic theatre to which we are accustomed is the stylized and rigidly traditional stage of which this marvelously graceful Oriental is both the chief exponent and ornament, that in venturing to come to us at all Mei Lan-Fang cannot but face difficulties that are unknown to the majority of visiting actors. For his native tongue is not the only barrier he must surmount. Nor is it, which is harder still, the only foreign speech that Mei Lan-Fang speaks. In truth it is but a part—and a comparatively small part—of the elaborate and exciting vocabulary which he and his fellow players have at their command.

For with them their gestures—like their words—form an independent language which is intricate in its syntax, infinite in its choice of expression, and which must be used purely, according to the strictest laws of grammar that is familiar to all educated Chinese theatregoers. With them, too, every movement of their bodies has a significance that is sufficiently eloquent to speak precisely to the knowing. Because, acting as they do on a platform which is bare of everything excepting a few mildly indicative properties, these players must set their stage even while they act, and establish the locale of each of their successive scenes by the manner in which they stoop at imaginary doors, or lift their feet after they have dismounted unseen horses, or travel in circles to show the long distance they have covered.

In the same way the costumes, the properties and the make-ups of these actors speak out boldly to their native audiences. In fact, they inform them so definitely as to the kinds of parts they are playing and the specific attributes they are supposed to possess that the stout volume which is handed to you as a guide at the Forty-ninth Street Theatre, is made considerably stouter by the long list of definitions it includes for the visual vocabulary of the Chinese stage.

In spite of the difficulties of that vocabulary, however, and in spite of the many subtleties in acting and staging which cannot fail to elude Americans who sit before this Chinese Company, the evening in the theatre which Mei Lan-Fang offers New York with his troupe is one of such rich and stimulating pleasures that more discriminating playgoers will be careful not to miss it.

With much wisdom Mei Lan-Fang has chosen five short dramas for his first bill, instead of one long play. In this way he not only spares his audience from fatigue, but exhibits the talents of his company in five dramas written in as many styles. In this way, too, he is himself able to appear in three plays, and hence in three of the feminine parts for which he is so idolized in the Orient.

Mei Lan-Fang employs the unreal, falsetto tones, which are the conventional tones used, we are told, not only by all actors playing female parts in China, but by actresses as well since they have been permitted to appear on the Chinese stage.

Though these falsetto tones may seem old and piercing when they first cut their way into untrained Western ears, it becomes clear as the evening wears on that as Mei Lan-Fang uses them, they are anything but a monotonous sing-song. Indeed, they come to have a weird, lilting charm of their own, if not a beauty that is inescapable.

Though it may take a little while to become accustomed to Mei Lan-Fang's falsetto, it takes no time at all to realize how rare he is as a master of stylization and how extraordinary are his talents as an actor. His acting shows his forethought and its surety in a hundred different ways—in the manner in which his gestures are completed, in the care with which his fingers are arranged for each new placing of his hand in the superb grace with which he manipulates his costumes, in the precision with which he uses his body, and in the design which is apparent in everything he does and into which his acting flows at all times. In addition, Mei Lan-Fang possesses amazingly expressive eyes and a mobile face that registers with the utmost sensitivity each of his passing emotions.

* * * * *

6. BY WHITNEY BOLTON

(New York Morning Telegraph, February 18, 1930)

The bill encompassed five small plays, in three of which Mr. Mei appeared, invariably as a woman. Not one was in the Western tradition, nor had one any remote touch with it. All were as sensitively and perfectly of their ancient origin as jeweled trees and court fabrics. It would be absurd to suggest that the complete sense of the plays could be followed with flawless understanding, indeed, except for the curiously engaging announcements by Miss Soo Yong, which preceded every number, much of which would have been impossible to follow. With these announcements, however, it was possible to follow Mr. Mei's own characterization and propulsion of the plots.

Mr. Mei's playing reaches perfection in grace, movement, the dance and facial expression. He conveys more in the turn of a wrist, the swish of a sleeve or the arching of the eyes than do most of our foremost actors in a whole evening of the less subtle and more forthright performances.

* * * * *

Mei Lai-Fang & David Belasco

B. LATER REVIEWS IN NEW YORK
1. BY ARTHUR RUHL
(New York Herald-Tribune, February 23, 1930)

To speak of Mr. Mei as a "female impersonator" is, of course, to give quite a false idea to those who haven't seen him and take the phrase in its usual American sense. He plays female parts, to be sure, but the women he represents are not actual, everyday women, but embodiments of the Chinese notion of the eternal womanly. His soft, undulating walk; the position and gestures of his long, slim fingers; the curious and often, to our ears, harsh, falsetto which, as the emotion depicted rises above a certain intensity, passes from spoken words to song—all this and much else is stylized and conventionalized into a ritual. Everything is a symbol, has its definite and understood meaning.. The actor, as a man, is merged completely in the design he is creating, just as the masculinity of a Sargent or a Gainsborough was merged in the portraits of the women they painted.

* * * * *

2. BY WILLIAM BOLITHO
(New York World, February 20, 1930)

Mei Lan-Fang, at the 49th Street Theatre, is indisputably one of the peaks of artistic interest in New York this season. His agent's claim that he is "China's greatest actor" very possibly is too simple a statement. For the character of his performance itself implies, I think, the existence of an extensive body of art and great number of fine actors in his own country. Among them it is likely that any classification by merit would be by indisputable choice. At any

— 39 —

rate, Mei Lan-Fang is of the first rank. In that convenient, if vulgar concept of sportsman, he has a place in the world team of the greatest figures of the theatre.

Before the mind starts on that terribly tempting game of comparison, if it has to, you should be quite clear that convention and the program have not misled you as to the particular art in which, whatever it is, he is a master. I think myself it is merely confusing to call this "acting." I do not know the least word of Chinese, of course. But his articulation is so distinct that every syllable can be picked out. And there are very few of them. In two of his selections from his repertoire there are no words spoken at all. And so, purely for the sake of clear thinking, and not with the slightest intention of slurring the Chinese drama, I suggest, that he (and his art) should be considered rather as a ballet even if it has to be a form of pantominic ballet which is quite distinct from any that we Westerners are accustomed to. To me, Mei Lan-Fang is above all a dancer; and as such I would not hesitate to put him in the very highest class.

There is an almost infinite number of delightful things to see, and, as I said, the intelligence has a share besides the eye. It is not necessary to worry about the exact significance of each gesture of the pantomime, which some learned critics have made a great point of. These little symbols were no doubt introduced at first for technical reasons of stage management. But they have now become delightful in themselves, dance notes, no more obtrusive or prosaic than those of any European ballet. For example, the maids of honor in his "*Vengeance on the 'Tiger' General*" walk around the scene to signify that it changes to another room. But this walk above its little meaning, is a dance, a swaying, rhythmic measure, like a cathedral pavan, with the rocking, exquisite step, as if the actors were only attached to earth on a moving pivot, which is one of the chief verbs of this manner.

In this same scene you will see the extraordainary heights to which the Chinese have brought the art of make-up. The "Tiger," who rules Peking after the Ming dynasty, whom Mei Lan-Fang rids the world of, in the role of the princess, is a symbolic representation in scarlet and lampblack of ferocity, cruelty, vitality, that leaves you gasping.

Perhaps of all that he does this Princess is the best—a study of beauty and art defending itself in desperation, as it must against the brute, like the most aristocratic and delicate of all fighters, the snake. Beauty has no natural arm against force but poison and ruse. But Mei Lan-Fang is master of other roles and other arms. In his sword dance from the "Heroic Maid," I consider calmly, he has reached one of the supreme possibilities. You will see this—this translation of the play of lightning and the winds in terms of humanity.

* * * * *

3. BY ROBERT LITTELL
(*A Playgoer's Notebook*)

Final week!—Mei Lan-Fang will give his last performance next Saturday. If you have not seen him, and do not take this last opportunity, some day you will be sorry. Some day your grandchildren, gathering round the plaid shawl over your knees, will shout down your ear trumpet, "Grandpapa, tell us about the famous Chinese actor and how he came to America and overcome the barrier of language with his delicate stylized gestures." And if you can mumble your praise of "The Drunken Beauty" and show them how the fisherman and his daughter rocked an imaginary boat, the little darlings will run away and let you go on reading "Fifty Years of the Theatre Guild."

4. BY GILBERT SWAN

(*Albany Press, March 23, 1930*)

Mei Lan-Fang, China's greatest actor, has established himself as the vogue of the winter season. Not since Duse and Bérnhardt made solo appearances has an individual artist attracted quite so much attention as "the pearl of the pear orchard." While the art of Mr. Mei follows an ancient classical pattern, this exquite dancelike pantomime achieves a perfection which the more esthetic writers have linked with the classical sculpture of the ancients. And, too, there is something of a thrill in a play which has had a run for 3,000 years.

* * * * *

5. BY JOHN MARTIN

(*New York Times, February 23, 1930*)

With the appearance of the distinguished Chinese actor, Mei Lan-Fang, and his company at the Forty-ninth Street Theatre the interested observer cannot fail to be impressed anew by the fact that the difference between the dance and the drama is one of degree rather than of substance. An exotic manifestation of theatre arts such as this provides an occasion not only to compare two points of view that are notoriously antipodal, but also to discover their many basic resemblances and, more especially for our purposes here, their relations to the universal principles that govern them in common.

Mei, himself, with that permeating quality which distinguishes genius, transcends the forms at his command with unfailing result. His voice itself, for all its falsetto strangeness, is of exceptional beauty. His physical poise and grace defy description, and it is easy to see why the Chinese critics burst into poetry over him.

Mei Lan-Fang, the idol of China, is declared by critics to be the greatest actor seen on the American stage since the heydey of Duse and the divine Sarah. The curious analogy between the art of these famous actresses and that of China's greatest actor comes from the fact that Mr. Mei plays only feminine roles.

* * * * *

6. BY R. D. SKINNEN

(Commonwed, March 1930)

The rather sensational success in New York of China's famous actor, Mei Lan-Fang, may be attributed to two things besides mere novelty or curiosity. His is an art derived from sources so ancient that it is bound to convey universal impressions. It is also an art brought into life with such minute perfection that it stimulates the direct response of mind to ordered beauty.

At least seven hundred years of unbroken tradition lie behind the conventions of classical Chinese drama. Certain gestures, certain details of costume and make-up and certain stage properties have come to represent certain well-understood realities as clearly as if they were printed labels. I understand that Mr. Mei objects to the word symbolism as describing these conventions and prefers the word patternism—largely because symbolism in western civilization has what he considers a cruder significance. He feels that Chinese theatrical conventions are the result of abstracting from a certain reality its essential pattern, whereas Western symbolism consists more in representing some object or emotion by some quite different object. It is quite sufficient to acknowledge that the Chinese drama seeks to convey the most universal elements of action and emotion, by not confusing them with particular time or place or form, and that this effort is successful even to Occidental eyes.

Mr. Mei's own work—which consists in portraying the universal elements in female characters—has the perfection of a highly traditional religious ceremony or dance. It is this perfection of execution, added to certain personal innovations, which the Chinese audience must admire, and to which a Western audience can also respond as it might to the perfection and style of an exquisite Chinese print. Mr. Mei creates images beautiful in themselves and not demanding a comparative standard of appraisal. His grace of movement is a universal grace. The detail of his gestures has inherent beauty. We are not asked, as in much modern art, to see beauty within ugliness. The sureness of his artistry surmounts the barriers which exist between East and West.

* * * * *

C. REVIEWS IN OTHER AMERICAN CITIES

1. CHINESE ACTOR WINS APPROVAL AT PRINCESS THEATRE

BY GAIL BORDEN

(Chicago Daily Tribune, April 1, 1930)

If you want an aesthetic thrill you owe it to yourself to see Mei Lan-Fang. For this gentleman demonstrates to perfection the victory of the art of acting over all other kinds of creations connected with the stage.

Consider yourself his conquest. In more or less meaningless plays, or rather, bits of plays, and with only the properties of gorgeous color and intricate beauties of silks and jewelry, Mr. Mei by the use of his cultivated natural gifts "overshadows a whole theater of others."

First by his incomparable grace does he indicate the loveliness or the coquettishness of the lady whose part he plays. There is none of your female impersonator, as we know him. But there is the suggestion of the feminine in every minute detail of voice and acting as Mei Lan-Fang interprets. An "impersonator" invariably overdoes the role in order to get it across, but in the Chinese tradition it seems to be only the subtleties of charm and manner which are brought to the fore.

Thus Mr. Mei walks and gestulates with a gracefulness which is followed from his sensitive eyes to the tips of the most delicate fingers you can hope to see. He is never impersonating; he always *is*. You sense this on his first entrance when, as a coy country lass greeting her husband on his return from many victories, he teases and baits the old fellow along until he is almost frantic. And most of the teasing comes through the eyes, the movement of the arms, and the pert inclination of the fingers.

The falsetto voice, a characteristic of the Chinese male doing the feminine role, is undoubtedly strange to westerners —and surely it appeared affected (which, no doubt it is). But in the little songs, suggesting a particularly keen spiritual feeling, you will have to admit that Mr. Mei carries in the weird lyrics, either a mischievous or sad sensitiveness, as the case may be.

It is out of the question for one unfamiliar with the innermost secrets of Chinese drama to endeavor to interpret its deeper meanings. And were they translated, I doubt very much if they would make you appreciate this Oriental artist the more. Like one who looks for the first time on a beautiful painting, not knowing the hidden meanings, there is the feeling, nevertheless of beauty, of a depth which surpasses its outward color.

As for color. I can safely say that never have I seen such a generous and gorgeous supply of it as in the Chinese plays. If you are interested in this alone you will get more than your money's worth out of the priceless raiment worn by the actors. Coupled with this, of course, is make-up. The general tone is naturally foreign to us, but when the comedian appears in a black, red and white face which looks for all the world like a mask but is not, and when the gentlemen appear as ladies, you are bound to gasp at the completeness of the llusions of beauty, horror and ribaldry.

* * * * *

2. 'ASIDES' HEARD IN CHINA FOR HUNDREDS OF YEARS

(*Los Angeles (California) Examiner, May 1, 1930*)

Eugene O'Neill created a furore in contemporary drama when he introduced the "aside" in "Strange Interlude."

Mei Lan-Fang, China's great actor, explains this form of exposition as an integral factor of Chinese drama for many hundred years.

The "aside" uttered by the actor in the presence of two or three others, is used on the Oriental stage to reveal one's emotion or secret. In Chinese drama, when the player is suddenly overwrought with emotion, he expresses himself by facial expression or pantomime; if the emotion is so complex that it cannot be portrayed in this manner, the actor lifts his sleeve, behind which he speaks or sings, or quickly steps to one side of the stage. Such actions make it clear that the others on the stage have not heard what was said.

* * * * *

3. BY GEORGE C. WARREN

(*San Francisco Chronicle, May 1930*)

As one grows accustomed to the conventions of Chinese dramatic art and the narrowness of its patternization, the genius of Mei Lan-Fang becomes more apparent; his power to transcend the limits set by the law laid down by hundreds of years of practice, and make pliable and mobile its granite rules more apparent.

Last night Mei began a limited engagement at the Capitol Theatre, presenting two new items from his repertoire of 400 plays, and repeating his superb exhibition of tragic acting in "*Vengeance on the 'Tiger' General.*" His pantomime, his control of muscles and nerves, his mobile face and meaningful gestures are here seen at their finest in the expression of the natural terror of a woman, however much she may brace herself to commit a heroic murder, at sight of blood and the body of her enemy, dead at her hands.

The story, like all the plots of Chinese plays, is simple; almost childlike and direct. The Princess to revenge the killing of her family, marries the rebel general who is responsible, and on their wedding night makes him insensible with wine and kills him with his own sword, afterwards cutting her throat to save herself from torture by his soldiers when they discover her deed. If he did nothing else than this play Mei would be called "great".

But he gives further evidence of his mastery in the art he practices by his delicate comedy as the mischievous maid in "Teasing the School Master." His face is a study in variety of expression, every fleeting shade of feeling, every move, every glance, has meaning. One forgets this is a man characterizing a girl. The assumption of feminine moods and actions is complete.

* * * * *

4. *Riverside (California) Enterprise* *(May 14, 1930)*

In an epoch when the trend is toward clear understanding between peoples, the American tour of Mei Lan-Fang has merited more serious attention than is called for by an enterprise purely entertaining in character.

Through dramatic art this actor has given America an intimate glimpse into the mysterious culture of his race—mysterious only because we know so little of it.

To pretend that an American audience can understand more than the surface of what Mei Lan-Fang has interpreted would be absurd, for symbolism and convention have been developed to so high a degree on the Chinese stage that an extraordinary and delicate quality of imagination and knowledge must be required to grasp its subtleties. Yet an American audience does recognize the presence of these subtleties and gains respect for a people capable of brushing aside superficial stagecraft and distinguishing the artistic features of a performance.

* * * * *

III. AN EVALUATION TWO YEARS LATER

Stage

AMBASSADOR IN ART

By Stark Young

(The New Republic, April, 1932)

I was looking one day at Tintoretto's "Crucifixion" in the Scuola San Rocco, that painting with its wild beauty checked and steadied by powerful thought, technical command and a fine abstract arrangement, composition that is completely expressive of the artist's idea. The lower two-thirds of the big space is crowded with figures, the cross on which Jesus hangs is on the vertical axis, his head touches the very top line of the picture. Below are various historical incidents, and the raising of the two thieves on their crosses, detail almost realistic, powerfully seen. A pyramidal group fills the foreground center, a triangle begins at the foot of the cross and moves outward and upward, broken at the edges with figures and trees. This picture has been compared to Greek drama, which is for once a most fruitful comparison, so uncommon in the criticism of painting. The realistic details, the figures, the actions, as in Greek drama, make up the base, and here the pity lies also. The theme is lifted high; that single figure on the cross, against the sky, turns all pain into a kind of metaphysical splendor and bare reason into the humility of prayer and understanding.

From this picture power, emotion and idea seem to bring us into a kind of eternity, which is the picture; but yet at the same moment under our eyes the whole life in it is reborn and awakens, and so—to use a phrase of 'De Sanctis'—and so in the eternal reappears time; something of the present and the future of our spirit moves in this great work of art.

At length I went out along the streets and to the piazza,

where I sat down at Florian's. It was here, resting it on the little table beside the coffee cup, under the cloudless sky of a spring morning, I opened my New Republic; the page was that with Mr. Felix Frankfurther's review of Judge Cardozo's book, and after a delightful beginning, I came to the sentence quoted from Mr. Justice Holmes:

"Of course the law is not the place for the artist or the poet. The law is the calling of thinkers."

Mr. Justice Holmes, noted for his learning and almost as famous for preserving through generations his charm and liberalism as Patti was for keeping her high C! I remember how that sentence came upon me, but almost any sort of taste would tell us that such reflections if set down now would be too personal both as to me and as to Mr. Justice Holmes. Suffice it to say I arose presently and followed the arcade down toward the Doge's Palace and into the piazzetta there. I stood propped against a column looking across at the Library of St. Mark's. I looked at that facade of Sansovino's, which I had looked at so often before; those pilasters and columns, the panels above and that sculptured frieze; the elegance, the invention, the superb learning and sophistication. How much of a spiritual indifference, an inexhaustible mentality, out of the Remaissance was there! In the morning light the endlessly varied figures took on a fresh life. I saw the intellectual rhythm of the design, quietly ornate, broadly sure of itself: sure too of those forms in it that arrested and held the fleeting glory of thought. All actuality had first been broken up, and in the artist's mind the visible and intellectual elements had been drawn again to each other, as if by a kind of love, and had moved toward the birth of a new life.

It is obvious that great artists gather up, cleanse with their creative joy, and create a body for whole epochs and cycles of the human race; and that by these works of art men have lived, found themselves, and from them gone on toward a new art that will express what has arrived to seek its own expression. Within this society of men diverse great figures from time to time have, of course, appeared; but it could hardly be said that law-thinkers had thought it all out before there was anything to think about or society to think for. In this respect their lot was at least the same as the artists', those unthinkers, all emotion, who needs must find, I should think, their favorite law-god in Justinian, who, with a weakness such as might have been expected from a poet perhaps allowed his laws to be suggested now and then by his beloved wife, a sometime dancing girl, shall we say, or if we shall not say, a former courtesan—the legal distinction between the two was not then so clear as it now is.

By this time, however, standing before Sansovino, and with strains of Dante and Cervantes at the back of my head, Mr. Justice Holmes' sentence seemed a little blurred. I could see it as largely a hangover from some bourgeois-Victorian point of view, whose culture included an esthetic theory that was muddled by the blood and bile of a stale Puritanism, an image of art that took in good faith Charles Eliot Norton's Dante translations (as art, so very like a refined British governess explaining Shakespeare in the servants' hall); and had a manly association with such artists as painted pseudo Greece, soft view of mountains, whimsies in water color. To temper the argument, however, I should say that while only the tiniest fool of a poet would even entertain such a distinction between creation and thinking as Mr. Justice Holmes implies, the silliest lawyer would agree with him at once.

The purpose of these remarks of mine, however, so ignoble in the presence of great creation in any line—poets, painters, lawmakers, architects, musicians, actors et certera—and possible to me, I trust, only in the leisure of a summer day, in streets where powerful and lovely abstract forms provide the nourishment of and bodies for ideas, the purpose is only to introduce a simple theme with regard to the Chinese actor Mei Lan-fang and his visit to America two years ago this spring. The immense success of that venture everybody knows: an unusually large theatre packed to the doors for weeks, a personal impression made by the actor and his companions that was remarkable and widely commented upon. Everybody knows also just now how much sympathy there has been, certainly here in New York and its press, for the Chinese cause. The point I want to make is that the art, the circulation, the manner and quality, of these Chinese artists and gentlemen may connect more than we might think with many people's attitude during the present situation. No doubt the economic elements involved have much to do with the American considerations between Japan and China, though precisely what these economic elements are seems a matter of contradictory theories and facts. We must not forget to allude to the economic nevertheless. Columbus, having shown his motives of finding a new trade route and of bringing back a gold earring or so, was free to spend the rest of his life creating a myth, glorious in dreams, lies and heroism, of himself and what he was like within.

I knew Mr. Mei, and the two scholarly gentlemen with him, Dr. Chang and Professor Chi, very well. I watched, and have watched since, the problem of people's reactions to the Chinese theatre that they brought. Some of it was doubtless town snobbery and following sheep, but much of it was a real admiration for so pure and beautiful and high an art as they offered us. Nor, half apart from art, was the mere expertness and skill of the performers without its keen or gaping admiration. There was another cause of this Chinese success, and that without any doubt. The presence of these three at the numberless receptions, dinners, teas and so on given everywhere in Mr. Mei's honor, both for genuine reasons and for drawing-cards in an overstuffed society, created very shortly a sense of them, of their perfect breeding, merry spirits and tireless willingness to explain their country and their art. Clearly to everyone, these were scholars, gentlemen, men entirely at home in art, which with them was a pure world complete in itself. The excellent impression thus created carried along to the theatre, and was a real factor in the growing friendliness and perception from audiences.

I not only think Mei Lan-fang the most complete artist I have ever seen in the theatre, fluent in all its forms; he seemed to me the purest spirit I ever met in the arts anywhere, a being completely artistic, expert, soundly human, simple, eager for such new forms and styles as foreign countries might show, but yet never for a moment confused by them; he, Dr. Chang and Professor Chi all understood and knew securely by the most profound intuition that nothing could be of use in China, no progress—if it should turn out to be progress—no new types, no anything, unless it be created anew according to Chinese tradition and the Chinese mind.

Mei Lan-fang had been accustomed to three performances a week, here he was obliged to give eight. He brought forty-five trunks of costumes and repertory of two hundred pieces; as I remember the line of trunks backstage, three of them had been allowed open, to dress only a small group of plays that must be given over and over to fit our system. He bore this stage strain almost to exhaustion, as he bore the endless entertainments, after his serene life in his own home in Peiping, as a poet, musician, wrestler, dancer, art collector, student of the classics. Before he left, he and his two friends were white-faced with weariness, though I heard them mention it only once. I am trying to indicate the extent to which Mr. Mei and his companions regarded themselves as ambassadors of Chinese culture and the great labor to which they put themsleves in this cause. You had only to see a half minute of Mei Lang-fang's in that passage in "The Tiger General" where the murder and hate came for a second on the masklike face, with complete knowledge of great tragic style, of generalized emotion made into fixed images, to know that such a man's idea of life scarcely consisted of endless mass handshaking. Handshaking between China and America was quite another matter. Meanwhile, his strong and exquisite and gentle character was spoken of more and more widely, and is still spoken of. The recollection of all this tact, breeding, intelligence and human friendliness in these Chinese gentlemen and the high art they brought, can do their country no harm.

* * * * *

PERFORMANCES OF MEI LAN-FANG IN SOVIET RUSSIA

PERFORMANCES OF
MEI LAN-FANG
IN
SOVIET RUSSIA

SYNOPSES
OF
PLAYS AND DANCES
SELECTED FROM
HIS REPERTOIRE

1935

Mei Lan-Fang

PLAYS

PLAYS

1. The Suspected Slipper
2. Fei Chen-o and the "Tiger" General
3. Revenge of the Oppressed
4. Madness by Pretence
5. The Rainbow Pass
6. The Drunken Beauty

The Suspected Slipper

The Suspected Slipper

— 1 —

The Suspected Slipper

(*Feng Ho Wan*, 汾河灣)

CAST OF CHARACTERS

Hsueh Jen-kuei . . . .
Ying Chun, his wife . . . . Mei Lan-fang

THE STORY

LIU YING-CHUN, the daughter of a wealthy man, fell in love and married a poor man Hsueh Jen-kwei against her father's wishes. In order to seek a career, Hsueh joined the army and was engaged in long campaigns and distant expeditions. He fought his way up and was appointed by the Emperor as King of Liao Pacification.

After an absence of eighteen years, he suddenly returns. Disguised himself as an ordinary foot soldier, Hsueh meets his wife at the door of the house, where she and her son live in great poverty. The husband and wife can no longer recognize each other. After the exchange of a few words, he comes to understand that she is his own wife, but in order to test her fidelity, he starts a flirtation with her whereby the woman gets angry and enters the house, closing the door behind her. Hsueh then reveals himself as her husband and is admitted into the house.

Being hungry and fatigued after a long journey, he wants to eat and to rest. The wife then goes into the back part of the house to prepare some food and a bed for her husband. Being not yet fully assured of his wife's faithfulness during his long absence, he looks around the room and finds a man's slipper under her bed.

When his wife returns, he wants to kill her, but Ying Chun seizes his sword and asks for the reason of his sudden anger. Hsueh shows her the slipper. She recognizes it as her son's, but retaliates by telling him that the slipper belongs to a person much younger and more handsome than he. Only after her husband has been exasperated to the limit does she begin to tell him that the slipper belongs to their seventeen-year old son, who was born shortly after her husband's departure. When the fond mother describes the appearance of the child, the father is horrified to realize that but a few hours ago he accidently killed his own son while giving an exhibition with bow and arrow.

He relates that, on his way home, he came to a place called Feng Ho Wan where he met a young boy who showed a rare deftness in shooting wild ducks. Suddenly a tiger jumped out from nowhere. In a hurry to shoot the beast, he wounded the boy by mistake and the tiger carried the young boy away.

He is overcome with grief and when the wife learns of the tragedy, she faints. Then they start out to find the body of the son.

NOTE

This short play is very popular with the Chinese public. The almost bare stage, the plain costumes, and the absence of mechanical devices, throw the entire burden of the play upon the actors themselves. In this piece, conventional motions are plentiful: to wit, when the hero brandishes a whip, it indicates horse-riding; when the couple stoop, it shows they are passing through a low door; when the man bumps his head against something unseen, there is an imaginary wall; the tiny block wrapped in yellow silk represents an official seal.

Fei Chen-o and the "Tiger" General

Fei Chen-o and the "Tiger" General

Fei Chen-o and the "Tiger" General

Fei Chen-o and the "Tiger" General

(*Tz'u Hu*, 剌虎)

CAST OF CHARACTERS

Fei Chen-o, a Court Lady . . . . MEI LAN-FANG
Ts'ao Fang-ts'ai, of the enemy forces
   and known as the "Tiger" General . .
Courtmaids . . . .

THE STORY

YEARS have not dimmed the memory of the valiant court lady, Fei Chen-o, who lived during the reign of the last Ming emperor, Huai Tsung (1628–1643). To-day Peiping residents still point to the spot where she is said to have avenged the royal family and where a peony, planted by her, may still be seen.

After the tragic death of the imperial family she had served, the court lady, Fei Chen-o, impersonated the princess in order to take revenge on the rebel, Li Tzu-ch'eng, whom the royal maiden was to wed. But when Li unexpectedly gave the princess to his foster brother, Ts'ao Fang-ts'ai, the "Tiger" General, Chen-o decided to kill the latter.

INCIDENTS IN THE PLAY

Having sung that hers is a desire for vengeance, Fei Chen-o proceeds to recite how kindly she has been treated by the empress, who has ordered her to wait on the princess and how the rebels have forced on the emperor and his family an unhappy death. She regrets bitterly that as none who has enjoyed the imperial bounty is ready to wipe out the disgrace she decides to do so by impersonating the princess. The foregoing facts are recited directly to the audience in characteristc Chinese stage fashion. When the blowing of musical instruments announces the arrival of the man, the heroine tearfully retires to don her disguise.

The prospective groom, Ts'ao Fang-ts'ai, known as the "Tiger" General, enters, tipsy from the wine which his fellow-officers have forced on him by way of congratulation. The female attendants summon Chen-o, now dressed as the princess. Ts'ao is delighted when the maiden lauds his prowess. He assures her that they will rule together.

The wedding ceremony is performed. While Chen-o sings of the nuptial candles, implying that theirs will be long years of wedded bliss, she persuades the man to drink beakers of strong wine. She cleverly has the two female attendants sent off on the pretence that she herself will minister to his wants. She also objects to his wearing armour on this happy occasion. Once more, she prevails upon him not to call the attendants but insists on helping him take off the heavy garments.

Having seen that he first gets into bed, she sings of the precious ornaments she is taking off. The beating of the second watch, 10 P.M. to midnight, is heard. She approaches the embroidered bed curtains and calls the man twice, and on receiving no reply, sings with emotion. "Brigand, receive the point of my dagger!" She stabs her victim again and again.

Loudly addressing herself by name and regretting her failure to kill the rebel leader, Li, she plunges the bloody dagger into her body.

The music of the play is known as the *k'un-chu*, a quiet style, in which the notes of the flute dominate. It is an art which flourished during the Ming and Ch'ing dynasties and which the elite of China to-day are making an effort to revive.

Ts'ao Fang-ts'ai is a *hua-lien*, or conventional type characterized by painted faces and the use of the full voice.

Revenge of the Oppressed

Revenge of the Oppressed

Revenge of the Oppressed

(*Ta Yu Sha Chia*, 打漁殺家)

CAST OF CHARACTERS

Hsiao En, an old Fisherman . . . .
Kuei-ying, his Daughter . . . . Mei Lan-fang
Ting, a retired Prime Minister . . . . . .
Private Guards . . . .

THE STORY

THIS is a story derived from the famous Chinese novel *Shui Hu*, or the "Water-front Rendezvous," dealing with the lives of more than one hundred outlaws, and Hsiao En, one of the chief characters in this play, is supposed to be the fictitious name of one of the outlaws.

During the reign of the mediocre rulers in the later period of the Sung Dynasty, oppression of the ruling class forced the stronger and unruly ones to highway brigandage. They sometimes clustered on hilltops or in some water rendezvous, taking law into their own hands and defeating government troops.

Along the shores of the Tai Hu (Great Lake), there resides an obtrusive person by the name of Ting. He is a retired Prime Minister and therefore is very influential in his native district. Seeing that the poor villagers depend on fishing for their living, he begins to levy an unlawful fishing tax.

The fishermen, though embittered, are powerless to resist.

There is an old fisherman named Hsiao En who is living with his daughter Kuei-ying. He pays fishing tax regularly. But on account of a long drought, no fish can be caught and Hsiao is unable to pay the tax. Ting therefore sends his underlings to force payment.

They arrive just when Hsiao is sipping wine with his friends on a fishing boat. The friends rebuke them and drive them away.

The underlings report the matter to their master and the latter at once communicates with the magistrate asking him to have Hsiao En arrested. Hsiao later surrenders himself and is reprimanded with forty blows on the thigh and is ordered to tender apologies to Ting himself.

Hsiao returns to the boat. He plots with his daughter for revenge. Both go to Ting's house on the pretence of offering a big pearl obtained from a monster oyster. They are admitted into the inner yards of the house. They kill the whole family of Ting and flee to Liangshan (mountain) and join outlaws.

INCIDENTS IN THE PLAY

1. Hsiao En and Kuei-ying are fishing on a small boat. They tie their boat under a shady

tree to enjoy a little leisure. Li Tsun and Ni Jung come visiting. Hsiao invites them to have a drink. Kuei-ying retires to prepare dishes.

Ting's servants arrive demanding payment of fishing tax. They begin to abuse Hsiao. The two friends of Hsiao are enraged and jump up, but are prevented by Hsiao from resorting to a fist-fight. Ting's servants flee. Hsiao En and Kuei-ying leave the boat and go home.

2. The servants report the case to Ting. Ting sends his band of trained fighters to force Hsiao to pay or to have him bound and brought back.

3. Early in the morning, Hsiao En is at home with his daughter. Then come violent knocks on the door. Hsiao orders Keui-ying to the back yard and goes to open the door. Encountering the trained fighters of Ting, he pleads that he has no money but will deliver it himself within a day or two. The trained fighters try to apply fetters and chain to the old man. Being himself a skilled fighter, Hsiao does not allow himself to be thus handled. The trained fighters then fall upon him as one body but are badly beaten and driven away. Hsiao later goes to the magistrate's office to explain the matter.

4. Kuei-ying is anxiously awaiting her father's return from the magistrate's office. She hears some one knocking and opens the door. Her father

tumbles in, wounded by bamboo blows, for the magistrate, at the beck and call of the influential Ting, has given him forty blows on the thigh and ordered him to tender personal apologies to Ting himself.

Kuei-ying weeps. She asks her father if he is going to Ting's house to make apologies. Hsiao tells her that he not only intends to go but will also take the opportunity to kill Ting's whole family. Kuei-ying asks to accompany his father. Hsiao rejects, ordering her to seek refuge somewhere before he leaves. Kuei-ying refuses to let her aged father go alone and therefore, they decide to go together.

5. Kuei-ying lingers as she is afraid that nobody will take care of the things in the house. Hsiao tells her that they may not return at all after entering Ting's house. Kuei-ying then cries. Both shortly leave the house and go to their boat which sails at night.

On their way, Kuei-ying again hesitates and her father tries to send her home. But she again refuses.

6. They leave the boat with weapons hidden in their clothes. They knock the door of Ting's house. They enter the house. Ting inquires what they have to offer. Hsiao says that the thing is precious and that there are two many people in the room.

Ting therefore orders his servants to withdraw. Hsiao En and Kuei-ying kill Ting and the members of the family. The trained fighters come but only add to the casualties of the eventful night. Hsiao En and Kuei-ying then leave the house in haste so as to join the "Water front Rendezvous."

Madness by Pretence

Madness by Pretence

Madness by Pretence

(*Yu Chou Feng*, 宇宙鋒)

CAST OF CHARACTERS

Chao Kao, the Prime Minister . . . . . .
His daughter . . . . Mei Lan-fang
The Dumb Maid . . . .
The Second Emperor of Chin Dynasty .

THE STORY

CHAO KAO, scheming Prime Minister of the Second Emperor, son of Chin Shih Huang, emperor and founder of the Chin dynasty, tries by means of wedlock between his daughter and the son of Kwang Hung to win over and form an alliance with the latter, who, being an upright and honest man, has often opposed his plans. But after the marriage, he finds to his disappointment that his daughter, who is a person of both astonishing beauty and remarkable character, becomes too loyal to her husband to render him any aid.

Desperate and bent on revenge, Chao hires a thief to sneak into the house of Kwang and steal a precious sword, called the "Yu Chou Feng" or the "Blade of the Heaven and the Earth," which the emperor has previously given Kwang Hung as a token for his loyalty. Having obtained this sword the thief is also to attempt on the life of the emperor with the very sword. The thief is caught and the sword is found on his body whereby Chao maliciously suggests that it is obvious that Kwang Hung has an eye upon the throne. The emperor banishes Kwang Hung to the far frontier while his son takes to flight.

Under the circumstances, Chao's daughter is forced to return to her father's home. While she is beseeching her father to draft a petition soliciting the emperor's forgiveness, when the emperor suddenly arrives. He sees Chao's daughter and is dazzled by her beauty. He orders Chao to send her to the court to become one of his wives. Being rather pleased with the opportunity to become more intimately related with the court, he at once acquiesces in the emperor's request.

Chao's daughter, as a loyal wife of Kwang Fu, Kwang Hung's son, balks against the plan, She is, however, afraid to incur the displeasure of the emperor. At the suggestion of a dumb maidservant, she decides that insanity is the only exit out of the jumble.

She is actually brought to the audience of the emperor as he has refused to believe the tale of Chao Kao. Facing the unscrupulous tyrant, and using various ridiculous gestures that seemingly vouchsafe her insanity, she enumerates the vices of the despot one by one. Disheartened and convinced of the real madness of the woman, he dismisses her from the court.

INCIDENTS IN THE PLAY

1. It is evening time. Chao's daughter is just pleading with her father for the purpose of extricating the Kwangs from punishment. The emperor suddenly enters the room. The girl quickly withdraws, but not before her rare beauty has been seen by the emperor. The emperor asks who the girl is. Chao says that she is his own daughter. The emperor thereby tells him that he is much pleased with her looks and wishes that he would send her to the court to become one of his wives. Chao looks pleased with the request of the emperor and readily gives his consent.

The Emperor departs. Chao's daughter returns into the room asking her father what has been said by the emperor. Chao tells her that she has been chosen by the monarch to become one of his favourite wives.

Astonished, she asks her father whether he has already given consent. Chao answers affirmatively and says that she will have to go to-morrow. The girl flatly refuses to comply with her father's order and the emperor's command. The girl retorts that the first marriage is arranged by the father, but the second marriage should be decided by herself, and that she has no intention to obey the command that comes from an unscrupulous despot. However, she is at a loss to know what to do to thwart the desires of the emperor.

Happily there is a maidservant, who, though dumb, is rather clever. She teaches her mistress to affect madness. The girl then scratches her own face, lets down her hair, tears open her clothes, cuddles her father as if he were her lover and her son and puts up a show that convinces her father that she has completely gone mad. The helpless father then orders the maidservant to take her inside.

2. The court opens with the emperor sitting on the throne. Chao Kao comes forward informing the emperor that his daughter has suddenly lost her mental balance and is in a dangerous state. The emperor does not believe it and summons the girl to appear before him.

The girl arrives. She has the full appearance of a mad person. She scolds the emperor and enumerates his various vices. The emperor is much enraged, but he does not wish to kill her. He dismisses her from the court.

The Rainbow Pass

The Rainbow Pass

The Rainbow Pass

(*Hung I Kuan*, 虹霓關)

CAST OF CHARACTERS

Hsin Wen-li, the General of The Rainbow
    Pass . . . .
Hsin Tung-fang, His wife . . . . MEI LAN-FANG
Wang Peh-tang, general of the Potters'
    Ridge . . . .
A Maid . . . .
Soldiers . . . .

THE STORY

TOWARDS the end of the Sui Dynasty in the seventh century A.D., China was thrown into a state of confusion due to the weakness of the central government. Many rebellious leaders established strongholds of their own to defy the government and to contend against one another for domination. The Rainbow Pass was held by Hsin Wen-li with the men of Potters' Ridge as their close rival.

In one of the engagements, Hsin was mortally wounded by an arrow shot by Wang Peh-tang of the Potters' Ridge. The widow was struck by the handsome manliness of Wang. She asked for his surrender with the promise of marriage. Her offer was spurned, so she entrapped him with a snare. Instead of killing him, the widow with some effort succeeded in obtaining Wang's consent which, however, was given only as a pretence. He was watching for an opportunity of doing away with a woman of such unreliable character.

The ghost of General Hsin appeared in the nuptial chambers, expressing intense hatred for the unfaithful wife. General Wang suspected the presence of the ghost. He killed the bride after a brief struggle. The pass was completely taken by the men of Potters' Ridge.

INCIDENTS IN THE PLAY

1. A messenger reports at the Rainbow Pass garrison that the men of Potters' Ridge are challenging a battle. General Hsin hesitates to accept the challenge for fear of leaving the Pass unguarded, but when his wife promises to guard the Pass and remain faithful to him even if he be killed, he goes forth to battle.

The two generals meet at the battlefield and after a short combat, Wang is defeated.

2. Taking as an emergency measure, Wang shoots Hsin with an arrow and kills him.

3. Upon learning the death of her husband Tung-fang immediately orders all officers to prepare for battle and revenge.

4. Tung-fang and Wang meet in the battle. During the combat, she admires him and compares

him with Pan An in handsome mien, with Wei Shun and Lu Po in military valour. She asks for his surrender with the promise of her hand in marriage. He replies that a soldier has his name to protect and amourous charm cannot bend his will. Tung-fang therefore entraps him with a rope and captures him.

5. On his way to the camp inside the Pass, Wang, now a captive, sings that his defeat is unfair and that, as the lady seems to be in love with him, he may be able to find an opportunity to escape. He tries in vain to solicit help from the two soldiers who are in charge of him. They break into a quarrel. Wang tries to free himself, but is finally subdued by the guards.

6. Tung-fang is alone, torn with comflicting emotions: sorrow for her husband's death and admiration for Wang's handsome appearance and valour. While she is absorbed in thoughts of love, her maid comes in and hands her a cup of tea, which she takes absent-mindedly.

Being not in agreement with her mistress's action, the maid persuades her to kill Wang to avenge her husband's death. Wang is ordered to be brought in.

When asked by the maid why she does not kill the enemy at once, Tung-fang says that Wang has no fault since her husband's death must be the will of the gods. She seeks Wang's consent in marriage, but it is refused. At the insistence of the maid, the lady takes up a sword to kill the charming prisoner, but she cannot possibly command her hand to do a thing which is against her will.

After some coaxing and threatening, Wang gives consent to the proposal, thinking that he may later obtain some opportunity of taking over the Pass and of killing this unreliable woman. He then asks for three conditions, namely, to hoist the flags of surrender over the Pass gates, to admit the men from the Potters' Ridge, and to make the wedding feast last for three days. The lady in her eagerness to marry him agrees to all of his three conditions and Wang is immediately set free.

At the feast the seal of the Rainbow Pass is transferred into the hands of Wang to indicate that he is now the leader of the Pass.

7. On the evening of their wedding day, when the couple retire to the nuptial chamber, the ghost of the first husband appears showing intense hatred for the unfaithful wife. Suspecting the presence of the ghost, Wang asks the bride to go to bed first while he himself sits up for a while. After careful consideration, Wang determines to kill the unreliable woman and to save his own good name. He then proceeds with his plan. The woman is

killed at the end of a brief struggle. The death of the lady means complete triumph for the men of the Potters' Ridge and, above all, just punishment for an unfaithful wife.

The Drunken Beauty

The Drunken Beauty
(*Kuie-fei Tsui Chiu*, 貴妃醉酒)

CAST OF CHARACTERS

Yang Kuei-fei . . . . MEI LAN-FANG
P'ei Li-shih, an Eunuch . . . .
Kao Li-shih, another Eunuch . . . . . .
Courtmaids . . . .

THE STORY

THIS popular playlet deals with Yang Kuei-fei, the most artful of China's four great beauties and the supreme favourite of the emperor Ming Huang of the T'ang dynasty, whose long reign extended from 713 to 755. Kuei-fei, who had agreed to meet her royal lover in the Pavilion of a Hundred Flowers, learned that the latter had not only broken his promise but had gone to Mei-fei, her most hated rival. Consumed with pique and jealousy, the beauty drains one bumper of wine after another until she sways about in a series of tottering dances. The slender plot provides a framework for the rapid changes in mood, dances of inebriation, expression of bitter jealousy, and dreamy wine-laden songs which hold for Chinese audiences a perennial charm.

INCIDENTS IN THE PLAY

1. Yang Kuei-fei, attended by her women and the eunuchs, P'ei Li-shih and Kao Li-shih, enters singing languidly that the moon, rising like the

Goddness Ch'ang-o from the Moon Palace, has flooded the world with dazzling brightness. She is joyous at the prospect of banqueting with the emperor. Having received homage from the eunuchs, she recites among other things that although there are three thousand beauties in the palace, her lord has bestowed all his love on her person. As is the common practice on the Chinese stage, she announces her name and tells the audience directly of her tryst with the Son of Heaven.

The eunuchs carry dusters of horsehair, which usually denote personages of divine origin, nuns, monks, recluses and so on, but which here are employed for the practical purpose of brushing chairs and furniture before the arrival of royalty.

The retinue make their way towards the pavilion, shifting their positions from one side of the stage to the other to denote travel in the conventional manner. The eunuchs call the lady's attention to the Jade-Stone Bridge, the ascent of which is indicated by wrapping the sleeve about the elevated wrist and stepping carefully with a motion suggestive of mounting. From the imaginary elevation, Kuei-fei looks down upon and sings of the handsome goldfish. She also is attracted by the swans overhead. Having sung in praise of the passing scence, she concludes as follows: ". . . We arrive at the Pavilion of a Hundred Flowers."

On learning from the eunuchs that the emperor has gone to the Western Palace, the apartment of her rival, she, in attempting to conecal her burning jealousy and wounded pride, orders one cup of strong wine after another.

2. When the favourite exits, the enuuchs move pots of flowers to decorate the pavilion. Here pantomime and the words of the eunuchs alone suggest the existence of the unseen pots.

3. Yang Kuei-fei re-enters with tottering movements and sinks to her knees when she hears that His Majesty has arrived. On learning that the announcement is a mistake, she can no longer control the passion which the wine has aroused and proceeds to make advances to the unfortunate P'ei Li-shih. Her next victim is Kao Li-shih.

The carefully arranged scenes carried out with the two eunuchs, who, in turn, occupy first one side of the stage, then, the other, incidentally reveal the Chinese fondness for balance, which is so marked in other artistic endeavours, notably in architecture.

When the eunuchs anounce that the hour is late, Kuei-fei, having once more expressed her displeasure with the emperor, dolefully sings, "I return alone to the palace."

DANCES

DANCES

1. Sword Dance from "The Heroic Maid"
2. Flute and Pheasant-Plume Dance from "Hsi Shih"
3. Sleeve Dance from "Ma-ku's Birthday Offering"
4. Spear Dance from "Ma-lan in the Army"
5. Dance from "A Nun Seeks Love"
6. Dance from "Liang Hung-yu's Victory over the Invaders"

Sword Dance

FROM THE HEROIC MAID

(*Hung-hsien Tao Ho,* 紅線盜盒)

THE sword dance is taken from the play, "Hung-hsien Tao Ho," or "The Heroic Maid" which relates of a fanciful tale of the T'ang dynasty (618–906). Two warlords, T'ien Ch'eng-ssu and Hsueh Sung, are at odds. The latter, determined to subjugate T'ien by methods more subtle than force, sends his maid, Hung-hsien, at night to his rival's bedroom. There the dauntless maid takes from the sleeping man's body a golden lacqer box, his most treasured talisman.

When T'ien receives the box returned by Hsueh and then realizes that his rival might have taken his life if he chose to, he gladly makes a friendly alliance.

At the feast given by Hsueh in honour of T'ien, the guest inquires of the man who has achieved the daring deed of stealing the box. When T'ien is enlightened of the fact that it was not done by a man but by a maid, he is greatly surprised. The host orders the maid to appear and she displays her skill in the Sword Dance.

Flute and Pheasant-Plume Dance

From "Hsi Shih" (西施)

Hsi Shih, a Patriotic Beauty . . . . . . MEI LAN-FANG
Hsuan P'o, her Companion . . . .

DURING the fourth century, B.C., The King of Wu, defeated the Ruler of Yueh, making the latter a vassal. Because it was known that the victor loved beauty, Hsi Shih, a village girl, was taught the art of dancing and sent to the enemy court. So well did she accomplish her ends that the King of Wu abandoned state duties in order to indulge in rounds of orgy and pleasure with Hsi Shih. Meanwhile, the Ruler of Yueh raised an army and inflicted on Wu a crushing defeat.

Hsi Shih and Hsuan P'o, her companion, entertain the King of Wu with a dance, in which flutes and pheasant-plumes are used for posturing. The poetic suggestion of the flutes, the rhythmic grace of the long plumes, combine to create a colour effect and a just position of patterns characteristic of Chinese theatrical dancing.

Sleeve Dance

FROM MA-KU'S BIRTHDAY OFFERING

(*Mu-ku Hsien Shou*, 麻姑獻壽)

BY MEI LAN-FANG

FROM the crowded pages of Chinese legend comes the celestial maiden, Ma-ku. In honour of the birthday of Hsi Wang Mu, or the Queen of Heaven, she has gathered rare herbs and made fragrant wine.

In the first part of the dance, Ma-ku offers the pot of wine on a tray. This is followed by a sleeve dance. The close association of song and dance is typical of the Chinese theatre.

Spear Dance from "Mu-lan in the Army"

Spear Dance

FROM MU-LAN IN THE ARMY

(*Mu-lan Ts'ung Chun,* 木蘭從軍)

CELEBRATED in song and story is Mu-lan, who, over fifteen hundred years ago, donned the costume of a warrior and went to fight in the place of her aged father. In old China, the motive of filial piety was as great as, if not greater than, patriotism.

In order that her father who had recently been ill might remain in safety at home, Mu-lan answered the imperial summons by wearing a soldier's uniform and going forth to fight the barbarians. For twelve years she remained undetected, saving the life of the generalissimo and winning imperial recognition for her bravery. A model daughter, she returned from the rigours of the field and her great triumph to put on her femine attire and to perform home duties in the women's apartments.

At the beginning of the dance, a few notes from a wind instrument suggests the neighing of a horse. Mu-lan sings that she has purchased saddle and bridle. In recitation, she relates that she has crossed the Yellow River and the Black Waters until white clouds at the horizon are all that she can discern in her straining vision toward home, and the rushing waters of the river make it difficult for her to recall the voice of her father.

The rapid strides indicate that Mu-lan is riding over a great distance.

The rhythmic movements and the posturing patterns of horse-riding are all suggested by the art of the actor with the help of the whip.

Dance from "A Nun Seeks Love"

— 41 —

Dance from "A Nun Seeks Love"

(*Ssu Fan,* 思凡)

AN outstanding musical monodrama of the Chinese stage, sung to the soft accompaniment of the flute and other instruments, in "A Nun Seeks Love."

Recitation, song, posture, and dance, harmonize to produce a synthesis that is typical of Chinese theatrical art. The duster of horsehair and the headdress indicate that the character is a nun.

The nun regrets that her life in the temple is a monotonous routine of burning incense and reciting sutras and that her youth may vanish before she has tasted the joys of love. She decides to escape from her unhappy seclusion.

After a few encircling steps accompanied by song, she has passed along the covered walk to arrive at the Lohan Hall. Her hands push apart the imaginary panels of the door, while she crosses the doors as she enters.

Looking up, she recites that to either side of her are solemn arrays of idols. By pantomime and song the maiden depicts various figures; one with his hands clasped about a knee, one with the palm of the hand supporting his chin, and still another gazing at her through weary eyes. She sings that the Laughing Buddha, Haitreya, smiles as if asking who will want her when she is old. She further contrasts the bliss of wedlock and the emptiness of monastic life.

The depression caused by dull religious duties vanishes instantly when she decides to seek the youth of her desire. Singing that she will take off her nun's robes and put away from her sight the holy books while she actually does so, the sad nun is at once transformed into a creature sparking with high hopes of life and love.

Posturing in the exultation of freedom, the nun sings: "... To-day I will go far from the temple; go down the hill to seek a youth. He may beat me, revile me; yet, would I not choose to become a Bodhisattva or to chant the sutras. ..."

Mincing steps indicate that the nun has descended the hill and gone out into "the world."

The dance of the finale is descriptive of the character's state of mind rather than of the actual occasion. At the same time, the dance itself pleases the eye, as does the richness of the costume. The latter, while following the general lines of a nun's garments, does not exactly conform to them in colour and quality. The situation vividly drives home the fact that the highly stylized use of the voice, the conventionalized grace of gesture and the display of costume are above all an effort to please the ears and eyes of the audience.

Dance from "Liang Hung-yu's Victory over the Invaders"

Dance

FROM LIANG HUNG-YU'S VICTORY OVER THE INVADERS

(*Kang King Ping*, 坑金兵)

THE play relates of events that happened in the Sung dynasty some eight centuries ago, when the country was invaded by the barbarians. In the camp of Sung there was a woman by the name of Liang Hung-yu, who, with her superb military skill and noble character, helped to repel the invaders.

At the beginning of the dance, she goes through the movements of adjusting her armour. Then, accompanied by dance, she sings that she is going to direct the battle with the singnals of drum beating and the waving of flags. Emotions of courageous decision and devoted love of her country are successively expressed by song and dance. She is now well prepared for the battle with the confidence of victory.

近代散佚戲曲文獻集成·名家文獻編 33
總主編 黃天驥

叢書編委會 編

梅蘭芳研究海外文獻集編（上）

山西人民出版社
三晉出版社

图书在版编目(CIP)数据

梅蘭芳研究海外文獻集編 /《近代散佚戲曲文獻集成》叢書編委會編. —太原：山西人民出版社，2018.3
（近代散佚戲曲文獻集成 / 黄天驥主編）
ISBN 978-7-203-10293-9

Ⅰ.①梅… Ⅱ.①近… Ⅲ.①梅蘭芳(1894-1961)—人物研究—文集 Ⅳ.①K825.78-53

中國版本圖書館CIP數據核字(2018)第017707號

梅蘭芳研究海外文獻集編

主　　編	黄天驥
編　　者	《近代散佚戲曲文獻集成》叢書編委會
責任編輯	翟麗娟
助理編輯	吉　昊
復　　審	劉小玲
終　　審	員榮亮
裝幀設計	謝　成

出　版　者　山西出版傳媒集團·山西人民出版社　三晉出版社
地　　　址　太原市建設南路21號
郵　　　編　030012
發行營銷　0351-4922220　4955996　4956039
　　　　　　0351-4922127（傳真）
天貓官網　http://sxrmcbs.tmall.com　0351-4922159（電話）
E-mail　　sxskcb@163.com　發行部
　　　　　　sxskcb@126.com　總編室
網　　　址　www.sxskcb.com

經銷者　山西出版傳媒集團·山西人民出版社
承印廠　山西出版傳媒集團·山西新華印業有限公司

開　　本　787mm×1092mm　1/16
印　　張　24
字　　數　200千字
版　　次　2018年3月　第一版
印　　次　2018年3月　第一次印刷
書　　號　ISBN 978-7-203-10293-9
定　　價　218.00圓（上、下）

如有印裝質量問題請與本社聯繫調換

《近代散佚戲曲文獻集成》編委會

總 主 編　黃天驥
編　　委　董上德　張繼紅　許石林　陳志勇
總 策 劃　越衆文化傳播·南兆旭

出版工作委員會

主　　任　胡彥威
執行主任　張繼紅　姚　軍
副 主 任　梁晉華　莫曉東
監　　製　徐　勝
委　　員　周　威　劉小玲　徐　勝　顔海琴　何　瀅　林旭娜
　　　　　張志杰　翟麗娟　王新斐　崔人杰　郭向南　史美珍
　　　　　魏　紅　吉　昊　薛勇强　解　瑞　秦艷蘭　張仲偉
　　　　　任俊芳
設計總監　李尚斌
設計製作　吴圳龍　莊生府　王秀玲

出版説明

一、《近代散佚戲曲文獻集成》鈎沉、梳理、選取十九世紀末到二十世紀中葉，散佚而獨具特色、頗具研究價值的戲曲文獻進行整理出版，以填補學術界在近代戲曲史史料方面的缺失。

二、叢書主要採取影印的方式整理出版，爲便於學界研究之需要，以忠實於原稿爲宗旨，對排版方式、原書內容的缺損、錯譌等均不做修復，在不影響內容的情況下僅對頁面的污損做了處理。

三、叢書作爲影印文獻，序言、附注、插頁皆予以保留，最大限度地保持原本原貌：單黑印刷的保持單黑色，彩色印刷的以原來的色彩進行印刷。

四、叢書分爲"理論研究編""戲曲史料編""名家文獻編""曲譜和唱本編"四大編七十册。

五、"理論研究編"主要選取了近代重要的戲曲研究名家絶版多年的重要著作。其中，或有部分重要經典著作後期有再版，如王國維先生的《宋元戲曲考》，我們選擇早期稀見之"正音學會校本"版，原貌出版。

六、"戲曲史料編"則對史材、檔案、傳記等史料進行了整理。"名家文獻編"對著名戲曲表演藝術家的文獻進行了集中整理，包括海外版史料、報紙雜誌或期刊的專刊、各種個人專集等。這些史料或散於海外、或沉於故紙堆，因極富時代特色且具有原真性，又長期遊離於主流學術研究視野之外，因而其研究價值較爲突出。爲保持文獻原真性，對於期刊圖書廣告頁予以保留。

七、"曲譜和唱本編"主要對戲曲的曲譜和唱本進行了整理。曲譜和唱本是戲曲藝術傳承、演變、發展的主要載體之一，近代的曲譜和唱本很多是當時演出的戲本，故不少史料具有民間性，對於戲目發展的原生狀態具有很高的研究價值，如小唱本，因非常零散，多年來幾乎未見整理出版。

八、因叢書主要採用影印的方式，故海外出版的外文版未進行翻譯，維持海外原版之狀態，適合較高層次的讀者閱讀、研究。

九、叢書中，因原版的零散或者底本的其他狀況不便於影印的《戲曲藝術散論叢編》採取了重新錄入的方式進行排版，由本項目組進行了點校、審讀。

十、對於篇幅較小的原本書目，叢書進行了合編出版；對於合編册數爲兩册的，保持了原始書名；對於合編册數爲三册以上的，則按整理的類別，重新編訂書名。

十一、所選版本的頁碼標註，在保持原始頁碼的同時，重新編排了新頁碼；對於兩册以上合册出版的書目，做了目錄，便於讀者查找閱讀。

十二、爲保證叢書體例一致，序言、出版說明、版權頁等附文，皆採用了中文繁體編排。

鑒於編者水平有限，有不當之處，敬請方家指正，又因出版時間所限，定有諸多不足之處，亦請廣大讀者海涵。

總　序

黄天驥

　　戲曲，是我國在世界藝壇上獨樹一幟的綜合性藝術。如果從金元時期戲曲趨於成熟的階段算起，歷經明清兩代，到晚清民國時期，它已經走過了近七百年的道路，發揮過重大的社會影響。

　　戲曲，包括雜劇、傳奇乃至花部小戲等體裁，在不同的歷史時期，其內容、形式，不斷地變化融合，也經歷過好幾個不同的發展階段。進入晚清民國時期，隨着我國歷史和社會出現翻天覆地的變化，戲曲進入了非常獨特的歷史時期。對於中國文化和研究中國戲曲史而言，這是具有特別意義並且非常值得注意的歷史時期。

　　我國戲曲，元代以雜劇爲主流，明清兩代，劇壇以傳奇爲主，也兼演雜劇。但到了清代乾隆年間，朝廷經常在爲皇帝、皇太后祝壽的全國性節日，引進各種地方戲班，進入北京會演。以此爲契機，徽班以其精彩的表演和它易於爲群衆接受的特質，在京城落地生根，影響日益擴大。它融合了其他唱腔，形成了後來被稱爲"京劇"的新劇種。這時候，各處的地方戲，風起雲湧。至於曾在舞臺上流行的雜劇、傳奇，即使在某些方面結合時代的潮流，有所革新，但終究敵不過以徽班爲代表的清新、活躍、更接地氣的地方戲。愈到後來，屬於"雅部"的雜劇、傳奇，漸漸無人問津，走向衰落。從此，"花部"終於戰勝了"雅部"，中國的劇壇，經歷了一次重大的變化。

　　從晚清到民國，隨着政治經濟的變革，西方各種思潮包括文藝思潮，也陸續湧入古老的天朝。我國戲曲領域，與中國人民反帝反封建的鬥爭相聯繫，與資產階級政治運動相適應，也出現了深刻的改良活動。以京劇爲例，劇壇上呈現出與元明清三代不同的面貌和特點。

從金元以至明清，我國戲曲經過長期的創造、沉澱，在劇本創作上，特別在唱、做、念、打等表演技巧方面，都在不斷地完善。乾嘉以來，商業興旺，中心城市如北京、上海一帶，市場繁榮，觀衆日多，審美要求也日益提高。加以宮廷的大力提倡，各個地方戲種有了交流借鑒、互相影響、共同提高的機會。以京劇爲代表的"花部"，特別在表演藝術方面，日臻成熟，達到了中國戲曲史上的高峰。那時候，戲班衆多，名角迭出。咸豐、道光年間，京師出現以演老生見長的程長庚、余三勝、張二奎。這三傑，被稱爲"三鼎甲"。後來又出現譚鑫培、汪桂芬、孫菊仙三位傑出的老生演員，被稱爲"後三鼎甲"。他們的做派唱工，或如黄鐘大呂，慷慨沉雄；或如雁嘯長空，悲涼蒼勁。他們風格各異，而其共同之點：品行端正，敬業不懈，嚴肅地對待藝術創造。因此，他們被藝術界公認爲偶像，也受到廣大觀衆的尊敬。

到民國初年，觀衆喜愛老生的熱忱，逐漸轉換爲對旦角的追捧。當時京劇湧現出四大男旦。梅蘭芳以俊美的容姿，唱、做、念、打已達爐火純青的表演技藝，讓觀衆如癡如醉。程硯秋擅演悲劇，以青衣應工，幽韻哀情，如泣如訴，唱到劇中的悽楚之處，讓觀者感同身受。荀慧生則表情多變，做派風流活潑，有第一花旦的美譽。尚小雲嗓音圓亮高朗，在串演女性角色中透露着英勃之氣，他尤擅演刀馬旦，在旦角中自成一派。那時候，"梅、程、荀、尚"，紅透了中國劇壇。

可以説，清末民初，是中國戲曲發展的高潮時期，尤其是在表演技巧方面，更是發展到藝術的頂峰。這一點，和戲曲在繼承傳統的基礎上，在新舊交替的時代，審美觀念出現變化，演員們在劇本內容和演技方面，爲適應社會的需要，積極地醖釀有所變化、有所革新有關。當舊的政治體制被推翻，崇尚個性的潮流湧入劇壇，"四大名旦"們，也就不斷刷新劇目，即使演出傳統舊劇，也注意作適當的改造，注意程式的創新，甚至懂得追求人物形象的個性化。於是，整個清末和民國的劇壇，出現了讓人耳目一新的局面。

在這階段，藝壇上有一個現象，很值得我們注意，這就是圍遶着名角，出現了一批在文學上或在藝術上很有造詣的追隨者。他們不是戲迷或跟班，而是對名角有着很大影響力的藝術顧問或参謀，在戲班中，他們在很大程度上起着導演、編劇兼評論家的作用。像齊如山、羅癭公、陳墨香等人，他們文化根基深厚，社會經驗豐富，對新思潮有所瞭解。他們的加入，對清末民初戲曲走向高潮，產生了積極的作用。

由於有一批高水平的文化人，經常與名角們長期深入地接觸，瞭解名角們的生活，熟識演員們藝術創造的過程，也和當時的優伶界一起沉浮。他們用文字把舞臺上下種種見聞記錄下來，從不同的角度描述當時劇壇發展的足跡，這就給後人研究清末民初的劇壇，留下了極有價值的文獻。本叢書的"戲曲史料編"，便是力圖完整地搜集這一時期劇壇有關史料，方便研究者對當時劇壇有詳盡的認識，也為人們進一步深入研究提供線索。

進入清中葉以後，我國戲曲表演，實際上已推行"演員中心制"，無論是京滬劇壇乃至各處地方戲，從戲班體制乃至舞臺演出，均以演員爲中心。越到清末民初，名角的作用越是壓倒一切。這樣的現象，在我國戲曲史上並不多見，也可以視爲戲曲表演發展到最高階段所呈現的獨特面貌。

由於演員表演的成就成了這一時期戲曲發展的標識，爲此，本叢書編選"名家文獻編"，輯錄了梅蘭芳、譚鑫培、周信芳等十一位藝術大師的文獻，其中包括演出報告、影集、雜誌、臨時特刊等文獻，以及社會各界對他們的述評和研究文章等等。通過此編，讀者既可以認識、學習一個個名角各自的表演特色、各自的藝術成就，也可以從總體上，綜合觀察這一歷史時期戲曲發展的趨向。

這套叢書，還列有"理論研究編"。

本來，從金元時代開始，戲曲已趨成熟，成爲人民大衆喜聞樂見的藝術形式，許多文人雅士，也參與到劇本的創作中，寫出了不少膾炙人口的名劇，被視爲"驅梨園領袖，總編修師首，捻雜劇班頭"的關漢卿，甚至還粉墨登場。但是，在戲曲理論方面，卻鮮有人認真思考。除了明末清初的李笠翁，寫了《閒情偶寄》，算是比較全面地總結戲曲劇本的創作和表演經驗的規律以外，幾百年來，即使是關心戲曲的名家，也祇作些蜻蜓點水式的評點，或者在書信中和朋友們發表些零星的想法，至多是在劇本的序跋中，涉及對劇本創作的思考。可以説，從古以來，我們傳統長於形象思維卻疏於邏輯思維的慣性，使古代戲劇家對戲曲缺乏系統性、學理性和歷史性的思考。

近代以來，國運日衰。隨着西方列強在軍事、經濟、文化方面的進入，我國不少精英人物，不得不考慮國家向何處去的問題。思想界和學術界的許多學者，往往在不同程度上，和西方學術有所接觸，直接或間接受到西方文化的影響，思維方式也有所改變。同時，他們也看到，與城市商業繁榮的局面相聯繫，包括戲曲在內的通俗文化，日益受到廣大群衆的歡迎，特別是戲曲的表演藝術突飛猛進，其影響甚至超出了國門。這種種因素，讓許多有識之士，再不把戲曲視爲不登大雅之堂的"小道"。這一來，戲曲理論的研究，逐漸爲學術界人士所關注。從王國維開始，學者們已把戲曲研究作爲一門專業性的學問。進入二十世紀的四五十年代，戲曲理論研究更成爲顯學。

當然，在清末民初，戲曲理論研究剛剛起步，但也取得了令人矚目的成果。後來，在抗日戰爭期間，在烽火連天、顛沛流離的日子裏，有些學者還孜孜不倦地進行戲曲研究，努力從理論上探索中華民族文化瑰寶的奥妙。有些學者追根溯源，探索戲曲發生發展的過程；有些則研究戲曲在不同時代的表現和特點，或者研究我國戲曲的形態；有人廣泛搜集和考索劇本劇目；有人致力於曲韻的研究；有人還注意對地方戲的論述，等等。可以説，清末以及民國時期的戲曲理論研究者，完全打破了傳統曲學評點餖飣支離破碎的方式，他們從不同角度，對戲曲藝術作系統性的研究，邁出了新的一步。即使有些地方，還待深入探討，但已爲後來的研究者打下了基礎。"篳路藍縷，以啓山林"，在我國戲曲研究學術史上，這一時期的學者功不可没。其中，有些論著，具有經典性，直到今天，依然是戲曲理論研究者必讀的文獻。爲此，本叢書設置"理論研究編"，努力搜集讀者不易看到甚至已經絶版的論著，意在既保存珍稀資料，又爲學者們開展對這一階段劇壇的研究，提供更全面的幫助。

經過多年的努力，《近代散佚戲曲文獻集成》叢書終於面世。這套叢書的出版，填補了近代戲曲學術史的空白，對推進今天戲曲創作、表演和理論研究，也很有價值。特推介，是爲序。

二〇一五年六月十二日於中山大學中文堂

"名家文獻編"序

許石林

一

　　大約十多年前的正月初十左右，陝西關中農村的年味兒正濃，我卻依依不捨地告別老家這片凝重古老的鄉土，要到南方去上班了。

　　途經西安，拜訪陝西師範大學藝術學院院長徐義生教授，茗談間，説起戲曲，徐先生興奮起來。當天叫了車，載着家母和我，從西安出發，經三個小時，趕赴渭南華縣，在我的老同學簡録民的安排下，徐教授出錢，請華縣當地的碗碗腔皮影藝人喫了頓飯，又給了幾百塊錢，請他們演出一場皮影戲。按照舊例，藝人們這時候應該封箱，好好過年，人來客去地應酬，但爲了我們的專程到來，他們破例在村外的養牛場空地上，搭起了戲臺，拉了電綫，天黑前點起數堆柴火。火焰很大，燒得通紅，入夜，火焰歇斂，剩下了幾大堆熾熱的柴灰，當地稱"火糟"，俗話説，"歇火歇糟子，喫饃喫包子"，這纔算是真正的烤火——烤火不能有火焰，容易傷人，這會兒主要是怕影響戲臺上照明唱戲。

　　不遠處就是秦嶺、少華山，山形如屏，隱約可見，一彎冷月，高懸於空，寒輝瀉地，萬籟俱靜，幽闃若太古。當地村民無一人來看戲，司機躲在車內聽歌，偌大的場院，就我們三個觀眾。戲臺後是五六位藝人。突然一聲巨響，人聲、鑼鼓聲破空而來："三軍們！嚇！各峪口嚴加搜查，切莫要走脱黄巢啊！嚇！追……"

　　"號角響金鼓鳴聲震山澗，揮金刀突重圍血濺征鞍……"——皮影戲《狼虎峪》，聽得人驚心動魄，霎時間忘記了身處寂寥的荒村野外，仿佛身臨唐末，群雄並起，刀光劍影。

《狼虎峪》開場，之後是碗碗腔的經典劇目，《借水·贈簪》《獻連環》《萬福蓮》選場等幾個戲。

白天和藝人們聊天，說起皮影戲長演不衰的劇目，尤其推崇清代劇作家、本地才士李芳桂的劇本。皮影戲簽手郝炳黎老人說了一個動人的故事：

李芳桂是清嘉慶年間的舉人，數次落第，遂絕意科場，專事編劇，共編寫了《春秋配》《白玉鈿》《香蓮佩》《紫霞宮》《如意簪》《玉燕紋》《萬福蓮》《火焰駒》八部大戲，加上兩個折子戲《四岔捎書》和《玄玄鋤穀》，俗稱"十大本"。戲曲自乾隆年間徽班進京，成為朝野時尚，發展繁榮，突飛猛進。自古以來，朝廷對文化有宏觀調控的習慣，道喪文敝則隆厚崇尚之；至風氣浮靡奢華，則減損裁撤之。戲曲經過了乾隆的大力提倡和推波助瀾，到了嘉慶年間，花部繁盛，販夫走卒，口能唱念，歌聲響徹街巷，以至社會風氣受到影響，人心向奢，朝廷遂對戲曲做了一番宏觀調控，裁抑地方戲。李芳桂因此受到牽連，連夜逃跑，竟然在倉猝之中，摔死在荒郊野外。作為"問題人物"的李芳桂，其劇作自然不能再演出了，劇本也不能傳鈔。相傳李家人是這樣傳承先人的劇作的：李氏家中婦女，每人每天夜裏紡棉織布，各人分工，在心裏默默地背誦先人的一齣戲，默完一齣戲，方許休息。就這樣，李芳桂的戲被傳了下來。據郝炳黎老人說："直到清末民初，某一天，渭北某縣的城隍廟有人到縣衙報告，說廟裏死了一個人，此人是流浪漢，但與別的流浪漢不同，他死的時候，頭枕着一摞書，城隍廟裏管事的因此不敢怠慢，才向縣衙報告。縣令抑或是縣長讓呈上那些書，翻開一看，發現是傳說中的李芳桂的'十大本'，但略有殘缺。縣令抑或是縣長令埋葬死者，自己將殘缺的劇本通讀一遍，根據傳說加以考據，又敷以情理將其補充完備。從那時候起，碗碗腔用的李芳桂（李十三）的劇本就齊全了。"

當時我十分震撼動心於郝炳黎老人的敘說，未便中途詢問，以免阻斷其語流，使其不往下講。要知道，村民質樸，如果多問，他怕在你們所謂城市人、文化人面前說多了失言，就會緘口不語。所以，至今，關於那個縣令抑或是縣長對劇本的保存補闕等情況，我無暇也無力去詳加考索。如今郝炳黎老人已去世數年，恐怕已無人能説明情況了。

由此可見，所謂繼絶學，需要有心人和緣分，且並非易事，稍微疏忽大意，綫索中斷，遂成千古之謎，遺憾無盡。

由此，想到整理出版這一套《近代散佚戲曲文獻集成》，真可謂一件讓人心動的事，於研究和繼承中國戲曲，不惟學問，尤其是功德。

二

戲曲文獻，大約涉及表演藝人的，晚清至民國，較前爲豐富。更早的，多闕失不記。這也是中國文獻向來鄙薄藝人的習慣所致。想象一下，倘若今天能找到一張元代演出雜劇的憑證，其價值恐怕相當於找到倪雲林的一幅真跡！

晚清民國，距今不遠，而戲曲從演出的内容到形式，都發生了與前大爲不同的變化。"劇曲之富，越邁胡元"，單以"同光十三絶"爲標誌的名伶薈萃，流派紛湧，可謂星光滿天，照徹後世百年。所以，文獻雖歷經滄桑，散佚毁損無算，但畢竟還能依稀找到，只不過經兵火動亂吞噬焚滅，曾經普遍，貴爲珍稀；曾經珍稀，罕成孤絶。今天中國人對彼時的戲曲藝人的資料，由於各個時期的歷史原因，公私收藏，多有散佚，或以爲不重要而未加珍視，所以很多方面恐怕不及外人重視。許多歷代查禁的"違礙"，在中國，或已絶跡，在别人，却多有收藏，甚至居爲奇貨。

《近代散佚戲曲文獻集成》的"名家文獻編"部分，所收集的名伶藝人的文獻資料，多爲民國，晚清幾無，如更早的程長庚、余三勝等那一代的資料，不見徵採，或已記録於别處，無復贅加。中國文字，向來輕視藝人，於此可見。這就更顯示出這些資料的珍貴。

中國戲曲百年前被外國人推崇備至，如日本人辻聽花，於清末民初旅居北京二十餘年，喜愛中華文化，尤耽於中國戲曲，"時入歌樓，藉資消遣。且與梨園子弟常相往來，談論風雅"，他與讀書人出身的伶人汪笑儂關係非常好，曾撰寫《中國劇》一書，動情高呼："中國菊國萬歲萬萬歲！"可見，他趕上了那時候中國戲曲演出最繁榮的時期。

這個時期戲曲藝人爭奇鬥艷，不僅承續"同光十三絕"餘脈並發揚光大之，而且成就了諸如以"四大鬚生""四大名旦"爲符號的戲曲演員群體。今天我們看這些史料，却明顯感覺，這是一個繁榮時期的一小部分記錄。地方戲曲想必也同樣繁榮，但却缺少資料。僅從這裏，可以想象那個時期戲曲生態的整體面貌。

分享梅蘭芳這位戲曲藝術家集大成者的演出特刊、《梅蘭芳歌曲譜》（五集）、《梅蘭芳戲裝錦集》等，可以想見，成就梅蘭芳的，不僅僅是他一個人的悟性、刻苦和種種不懈的努力，而且是一個團隊的成功合作。其工作之細緻周到，令人嘆爲觀止。

再以《程硯秋赴歐洲考察戲曲音樂報告書》爲例，可見當時藝人競爭的激烈。與梅蘭芳赴美國演出獲得轟動相得益彰。梅、程之間的師友之爭，向來是喜好梨園歷史的人談論的話題。却因爲缺少第一手資料，而多數淪爲人云亦云、捕風捉影、妄意揣測。筆者曾經與程硯秋先生的三子程永江先生有交往，永江先生坦言，程硯秋先生心氣高、肯下功夫、有心機，同時也多疑。筆者聞聽此言，當時感覺，這恐怕是當時藝人被生存逼出來的性格，如果沒有那種内在的發狠較勁，恐怕一個中途壞了嗓子的程硯秋，會被湮没在當時的氛圍中。

因此，通過這些史料，回頭再看梨園界精英們的競爭，造就了當時戲曲的繁榮，給後人留下了精湛絕倫的藝術遺産。

三

通觀這些史料，給人的啓迪如下：

晚清民國戲曲舞臺的繁榮，藝人們長袖善舞，但其表演的内容和市場運作，却是以讀書人爲核心甚至主導的。不僅有齊如山、羅癭公、陳墨香、金仲蓀諸賢與藝人深度合作,他們自己的人生,遭遇神州陸沉之變,無法施展,遂流連氍毹,假借藝人之口,於舞臺天地,表達其家國天下的治世情懷。就連馬相伯、于右任等,也都是與戲曲藝人有深厚交情的師長益友,所謂捧角兒之風雅,於此可知。今天的戲曲演員,翻看這些史料,當悵然仰天長嘆。

其時正是新戲紛出的時期,藝人們所編演新戲,即便如梅蘭芳的《一縷麻》、尚小雲的《摩登伽女》等時尚戲,也無不在中華傳統的文化價值觀之中,即當時的編劇和表演藝術家,基本沒有拋棄本該萬古不易的中華傳統文化價值,帝王將相、才子佳人所承擔的高臺教化功能,傳播的也是這種價值,萬變未離其宗。如李萬春編演《投筆從戎》,也是忠實地遵循《後漢書》。亦可見當時的觀衆,願意接受花部戲曲所傳遞的習慣價值,而不是盲目追求時尚,以期背叛主流、趨附新異。

史料中有不少是當時的臨時性刊物,並非專著。這些臨時刊物,編寫精湛,文辭雅潔,多出自當時文章妙手,且有許多商業廣告。這是當今許多人想不到的。其製作精良,編排得體,足見當時人的思想之開放活躍。這讓人想起一個重要的問題,多年來較少有人關注關心晚清民國時期的戲曲生態,即戲曲是如何生存和繁榮的。並非如今天的文化經營者尤其是文化管理者所認爲的那樣,將戲曲推向市場賣票就會萬事大吉。其實當時,即便是在北京、上海這樣的大城市,戲曲的生態主要還是延續了中國戲曲一直以來"一人花錢,百家看戲"的模式,或將其衍化成各種形式,以演出前的團隊營銷、贊助爲主,而非簡單的售票,每一個角兒的背後,都有各自的金主,彼此義利轉化的交情。這種文化生態,是爲今天所忽視了的。

史料是一個生態,它的價值在於爲後人的研究提供了翔實的依據。

翻閱這些文字,讓人不時滋生慚愧之感:與前人比,在某些方面,今人是退化了的。

但是,看這些史料,明顯有一個遺憾,即地方戲曲的資料太少。我曾經爲此欲諮詢陝西渭南的戲曲研究家曹先生，希望能獲得一些他所掌握的有關資料。一經聯繫，得知曹先生剛過古稀，却已去世，不能不讓人滋生"欲問其事，而故老盡矣"之嘆。

回想戲曲在晚清民國時期曾經的繁華，一個時代有一個時代的風尚和潮流，但正如張中行先生曾説的："潮流是很少迴流的。"閲讀這些史料，已故戲曲藝人以及圍遶他們的前輩士子，音容笑貌，如在眼前。

前塵未遠，往事如煙，清末民初那些脆薄的紙張，經過仿舊如舊的印刷，帶着前人的氣息和味道，重新呈現在後世人面前，往史得以延年，絶學待有緣人去承繼，這正是這些史料重新出版的價值，它不一定能熱銷成爲時尚，但畢竟使許多往史故實，有了更多的接觸後人的機會，今後，鍾情於國故、熱愛戲曲的人，看到這些出版物，有多少人會掩卷唷嘆："當日裏好風光忽覺轉變！"

二〇一五年七月十日

MEI LAN-FANG
Foremost Actor of China

Mr. Mei Lan-fang

MEI LAN-FANG

Foremost Actor of China

Printed at
The Commercial Press, Limited
Shanghai, China
1929

Ad Interim Copyright in the United States by
George Kin Leung, December, 1929

All Rights Reserved

FOREWORD

It is a rare pleasure to be allowed to write a few words of introduction to this timely little volume. In addition to what it tells of personal interest regarding its celebrated subject, it also imparts just the sort of information that Western readers need to have about the history and technique of histrionic art in China. If to readers unfamiliar with China the praise of Mr. Mei seems to be tinged with oriental extravagance, they can be assured that the author's estimates and encomiums truly represent the popular opinion of all classes among this people regarding their gifted fellow-countryman. Not only so, but foreigners also fall under his spell, although unable to analyze the source of his charm. The merit of this book for us is that it aids towards a more intelligent appreciation of the exquisite grace and consummate art of an actor whose witchery fascinates us even when we miss the subtle meanings and delicate nuances so appealing to his Chinese audiences.

Any comment about Mr. Mei Lan-fang would, however, be incomplete if concerned only with his professional attainments, for in private life he is an attractive young man of gentle culture, unspoiled by all the adulation lavished upon him and with an almost naïvely responsive friendliness. Even in a land where hospitality is an accomplishment, he is the more delightful as a host because he then is never acting. He has a generous readiness to share alike the mastery of his art and its financial profits with those who can benefit thereby.

J. LEIGHTON STUART.

PREFACE

Prefaces, at their best often boring, are sometimes necessary. This is especially true, when, as in this case, the material of the volume has been compiled from many Chinese sources, and one attempts to mould the results, along with his own investigations, into an English book. The preface naturally falls into two divisions: (1) Miscellaneous remarks; and (2) acknowledgments.

1. Perplexing problems were encountered in Chapter VI and elsewhere, for there were no English newspaper cuttings to be had and all available facts had already been translated into Chinese, thus bringing about certain modifications. So, when the Chinese was once more rendered into English, further changes may have been made. This will explain why the interviews, critiques, etc., differ from the originals. Again, all European and Japanese names had been transliterated into Chinese, and were often impossible to identify.

2. It is a pleasure and a privilege to make acknowledgment to those who, gifted in their own right, devote their efforts to furthering the work of their friends. With this foremost in mind, I wish to express my sincere thanks to the following friends, who have made this English version possible:

To Mr. George T. Moule, my literary guide, who has accomplished the difficult task of reading two different versions of the manuscript.

To a family group, the Laws and the Kuans. Mr. Henry K. C. Law, who introduced me to the Peking drama, has given much practical assistance, while Mrs. Law has written much of the Chinese. Her brother, Mr. Heyward Kuan, reviewed with me, during the warm summer days, the original Chinese records.

To Mr. D. J. Kajiwara, who romanized the Japanese names.

To Miss Alice M. Roberts, of the Commercial Press, who is both an expert proof reader and an invaluable adviser in matters relating to the make-up of my books.

GEORGE KIN LEUNG.

PEKING (PEIPING), May, 1929.

CONTENTS

CHAPTER I
The Theatre of the Chinese People

The Living Theatre — Art of Mr. Mei Lan-fang as an Approach to the Chinese Theatre — An Old-Fashioned Chinese Playhouse — Training School — "One Touch of Nature" — Struggle for Existence Among Actors . . 5-7

CHAPTER II
Memoirs of Mr. Mei Lan-fang

A Chinese Literary Fancy — Ancestral Home — Grandfather, Mr. Mei Chiao-ling — Birth — Début at Twelve — Success in Shanghai — Voted "Great King of Actors" — Two Triumphal Tours of Japan — Cities of China — Hobbies — Exercise — Offices — Audience with the ex-Emperor, Hsüan T'ung — Disciples of the Pear Orchard — A First Impression of the Actor — The Social Yoke 11-13

CHAPTER III
The Female Impersonator of the Chinese Stage

New Movements and Old — Why Men Portray Feminine Rôles — The Actress, Her Suppression and Return, Her Plight To-Day — Attitude Towards Men and Women Appearing Together — Impersonators of Other Lands, Shakespearean Times — Performance of *Kuei-fei Intoxicated with Wine* by Mr. Mei — The Falsetto — Six Conventional Character Stage Types — Considerations of the Operatic, Histrionic, Gymnastic, and Comic in Feminine Rôles 17-23

CHAPTER IV
Mr. Mei's Contributions to Chinese Drama

Chinese Audiences — Question of Preservation of and Departure from Convention — Revival of Old Plays — Flute and *Hu-ch'in*, or Chinese Violin — Reinstatement of Musical Instruments and Head-Dress — The Mei School, or Ancient Costume Drama — Dance Creations — Ancient Dress — Plays Based on the Novel *Hung Lou Mêng* — School for the Study of Dramatic Art

CONTENTS

Dramas Produced by Mr. Mei Lan-Fang:
    The Love of Têng Hsia Ku — *The Imprisoned Lovers* — *Ch'ang O's Flight to the Moon* — *Tai-yü Burying the Blossoms* — *A Strand of Flax* — *A Beauty's Smile* — *The Heavenly Maiden Scattering Flowers* — *Mu-lan in the Army* — *Ma Ku Offering Birthday Gifts* — *A Young Girl Kills a Serpent* — *Hung Hsien's Theft of the Box* — *The Goddess Shang Yüan* — *The King's Parting with His Favourite* — *The Patriotic Beauty Hsi Shih* — *Beauty in a Fisherman's Net* — *The Goddess of the River Lo* — *Yang Kuei-fei* 27-36

CHAPTER V

Representative Dramas of Mr. Mei

Frequency of Appearance of Actors in Peking and Shanghai — Repertoire — Problems Faced by Actors — Public Taste — Conventional Types Impersonated by Mr. Mei Lan-fang — *The Fateful Sword* for an Operatic Heroine, Stressing Old-Time Morality and Characteristics of Peking Drama — *Histrionic Heroines* as an Intoxicated Beauty, Maidservants, etc. — *The Heavenly Maiden Scattering Flowers*, for an Ancient Costume Heroine, with Comments on the Art of Chinese Dancing — *The Jade Hairpin*, for the Heroine who Sings to the Accompaniment of the Flute — *Rainbow Pass*, for a Military Heroine, with Comments on a Stage Battle — Two Plays from the Novel *Hung Lou Mêng*, *Tai-yü Burying the Blossoms*, and an Example of Transitional Drama, *Charming Hsi-jên* . 39-51

CHAPTER VI

The Foreign Friends of Mr. Mei Lan-fang

Dr. Rabindranath Tagore — Sir Claude Severn — The Crown Prince and Princess of Sweden — Madame Galli Curci — Mr. Rudolph Friml — Mr. Frank Hedges — Baron Okura — Miss Kakuko Murata — Mr. Morita — Addresses Delivered by Messrs. Mei Lan-fang, Morita, and K. K. Feng 55-61

CHAPTER VII

Mr. Mei Lan-fang in Chinese Eyes

How Chinese Critics Say It — An Encomium — A Catalogue of Merits by Mr. Hsiu Mo — Throng of Admirers in Hangchow — An Opening Night in Shanghai — Pleasures and Trials of a Celebrity — A Day in the Actor's Life 65-73

APPENDIX 81-121

INDEX 125-132

LIST OF ILLUSTRATIONS

Mr. Mei Lan-fang

Mr. Mei Impersonating a Manchu Princess

Mr. Mei's Painting: Birds and Bamboos

Mr. Mei Chiao-ling, the Actor's Grandfather

Mr. Mei Yu-tien, Mr. Mei's Paternal Uncle

Mr. Mei and His Grandmother

Mr. Mei Chu-fen, Mr. Mei's Father

The Actor in His Garden

The Actor in His Library

Mr. Mei as Mu Kuei-ying

In the Dress of a Poverty-Stricken Woman

Impersonating the Maidservant, Ching-wên

In the Male Attire of a Warrior in *Mu-lan in the Army*

Mr. Mei Lan-fang in *The White Snake*

Hsi Shih, the Patriotic Beauty

Lien Ching-fêng as She Appears in a Marine Battle

The Goddess of the River Lo

Yang Kuei-fei as Portrayed by Mr. Mei

Mr. Mei as the Heavenly Maiden

Chen Miao-ch'ang, the Heroine of *The Jade Hairpin*

Miss Ruth St. Dennis, Mr. Mei, and Mr. Ted Shawn

Mr. Mei in a Joint Programme with Miss Ruth St. Dennis and Mr. Ted Shawn

The Crown Princess Louise Alexandra and the Crown Prince Gustavus Adolphus of Sweden, with Mr. Mei

Mme. Galli-Curci and the Actor in the Mei Gardens

Mr. Mei and Some of His Foreign Friends

LIST OF ILLUSTRATIONS

The Actor Between Sir Miles Lampson and Lady Lampson

Mr. Mei with Mr. John Van A. MacMurray

Mr. Mei and Some of His Friends

Mr. Mei and Sir Robert Lorraine

The Actor in Chinese Dress

Mr. Mei in European Attire

A Red-Lacquered Colonnade Leading to the Mei House

Mr. Mei's Painting: The Bodhisattva P'u-hsien

Facial Paintings, Ming Period

Stage Representations of Lesser Deities and Supernatural Beings, Ming Period

Stage Heroes as Painted in the Ch'ing Dynasty

Examples of Facial Painting Now on the Peking Stage

Styles of Present-Day Facial Painting

Costumes of the Chinese Stage

Headgear

Beards

Stage Properties and Symbolism

Stage Weapons

Musical Instruments

MEI LAN-FANG

NOTE

I wish our readers to bear in mind that the general outline of this book was compiled *in Chinese* by admirers of Mr. Mei Lan-fang. What originally had been intended to be Chapter III, which proved to be a dictionary of theatrical terms, has, in the present brief English volume, been made the Appendix. Of the Chinese of this part of the book, Professor Chi Jushan wrote seven divisions, and Mr. Huang Chiu-yao, two.

Chapters I, III, and V are the results of my own investigation; other chapters contain data from the Chinese records which the friends of the actor, notably Professor Chi Jushan and Mr. Huang Chiu-yo, have been keeping for some years.

GEORGE KIN LEUNG.

THE THEATRE OF THE CHINESE PEOPLE

Mr. Mei Impersonating a Manchu Princess

MEI LAN-FANG

CHAPTER I
THE THEATRE OF THE CHINESE PEOPLE

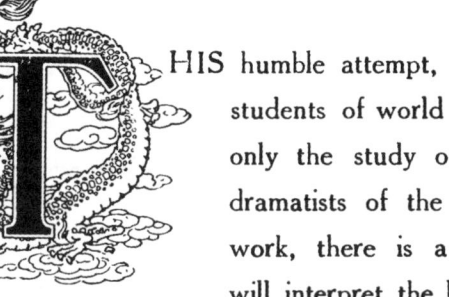THIS humble attempt, it is hoped, will lead more students of world drama to be discontent with only the study of books. While critics and dramatists of the closet variety do admirable work, there is a crying need for men who will interpret the living theatre. Once, after a youthful Chinese professor had read a scholarly paper on the drama, one of the many foreigners present asked him which playhouse in the city was worth visiting. The speaker shamefacedly confessed that he had never been to one.

While the condemnation of the closet method of study is not of first importance, of immediate concern it is to choose some factor about which to group the outstanding characteristics of the Chinese theatre. What well supplies this need is the art of Mr. Mei Lan-fang, the brilliant theatrical idol whose name exerts over the Middle Kingdom a magical influence. About him will be created a picture of the theatre here to-day, though no attempt will be made to exhaust the many phases of this vast field; such an effort would furnish material for years of research.

Let us, then, without further delay proceed to the Kuangho Lou, a theatre in the amusement district of Peking just outside the Ch'ien Mên. An actor assures one that he comes from Peking even if he were born elsewhere, just as, in the not distant past, all hats came from Paris, or at least so the labels said.

A noble example of an old-style theatre, the Kuangho Lou holds its own against the competition of both the modernized Chinese playhouse and the motion picture. There is much that meets the eye of the foreigner on his first visit. What he sees points out that, while in detail the East may differ from the West as Tientsin from Toronto, the fundamental idea of mass enjoyment is the same the world over.

Everything is strangely new and attention-compelling. Children — all boys, for this is a training school for male performers — act not only the rôles of bearded generals but also those of dainty, flower-like maidens. Loudly applauded by the spectators, the miniature monks, demi-mondaines, lovers, and acrobats pace across the platform stage, which, perhaps, is the only living likeness of that of the Shakespearean era. Running at right angles to the front of the stage are long tables, at which, about twenty deep on either side, sits most of the audience. Ears rather than faces are toward the actors, because in an old-fashioned playhouse one goes to hear a drama. It is a curious coincidence that there were in London, about 1600, two training schools for boy-actors, just as to-day in Peking there are two leading institutions with their respective theatres in which boy-performers make their appearances.

A conventional comedian type, or *ch'ou*, now caricaturing a Buddhist monk, recites "gags" which are both laughable and *risqué*. He gathers from the audience one round of laughter and applause after another. The merriment strikes in the foreign visitor a responsive chord, although but a moment ago he had thought he had nothing in common with his surroundings. A seductive siren exercises her every charm to batter down the moral resistance of a youthful scholar; an actor, in a rôle otherwise serious, pauses long enough to display his acrobatic skill as might be done in certain old French classics; these and other touches which link the present scene to the great mimic world outside gradually cause the onlooker to feel at home in this theatre on the opposite face of the earth.

The Kuangho Lou not only introduces one to a conservative Peking audience but also affords a glimpse of the very cradle of the theatrical profession. From such institutions, hundreds of graduates go forth to earn their daily rice; but since the supply is far greater than the demand, many of the profession live from hand to mouth.

Out of this heart-rending competition, Mr. Mei Lan-fang has risen to a position of overwhelming popularity. The approach to the living theater will, therefore, be made through this actor, whose artistry captivates alike the illiterate and the learned — in short, the teeming millions of the Republic of China.

To know their theatre is to know, in no small degree, the Chinese people.

Birds and Bamboos — a painting by Mr. Mei Lan-fang

MEMOIRS OF MR. MEI LAN-FANG

The Actor's Grandfather, Mr. Mei Chiao-ling, Impersonating an Empress Dowager

Mr. Mei's Paternal Uncle, Mr. Mei Yu-tien, Foremost Musician of His Day, who Reared the Actor after the Death of the Latter's Father

Mr. Mei Lan-fang and His Grandmother

The Father of China's Theatrical Idol, Mr. Mei Chu-fen

CHAPTER II
MEMOIRS OF MR. MEI LAN-FANG

THE supreme favourite of the Chinese stage, Mr. Mei Lan-fang, tempts one to hold the delightful fancy that certain kinds of earth, hills, and water combine to produce rare examples of talent and beauty. The spectator, after falling under the spell of Mr. Mei's acting, should therefore bear in mind that the artist's success is, in part, due to two distinct factors: his ancestral home, Taichow, Kiangsu, a region famed for its fair inhabitants; and noble Peking, the training place of the nation's best actors. In the latter city, his family has lived for three generations.

Idols of the court and of the people were Mr. Mei's ancestors. His grandfather, Mr. Mei Chiao-ling, remembered for his talent and proverbial kindness, was the head of the Ssŭ-hsi Training School for Actors, the leading institution of the four during the Hsien Fêng period (1851-1861).

October 22, 1894, is the authentic date of Mr. Mei Lan-fang's birth. At the age of eleven, the artist made his professional début as a *tan*, or actor of female rôles. Seven years later, he gained an unprecedented popularity in Shanghai. Afterwards, Peking, that most fastidious judge of dramatic art, by a vote of two hundred and seventy thousand proclaimed the youth the "Great King of Actors."

On Mr. Mei's arrival in Tokyo in 1917, thousands of people, eager for a glimpse of him, thronged the railway station. His second tour of Japan in 1924, when he was honoured by a request to appear in the newly reopened Imperial Theatre, was also a marked success. In the orient, Hongkong, Canton, Tientsin, Hankow, Hangchow, and Shanghai have, in turn, laid tribute at the feet of the public idol.

Gardening, entomology, and modern inventions hold for the artist a strange fascination. The Mei library is filled with rare old Chinese books and treatises on music and the dance, which frequently furnish the bases of his operatic dance dramas. The better motion pictures find in the actor a steady patron. Gymnastics and difficult forms of Chinese boxing keep him physically fit.

Mr. Mei, who is president of the Peking Actors' Association and who was the president of the Actors' Theatrical Association, was summoned in 1923 by the ex-emperor Hsüan T'ung to appear in the Yang Hsin Palace of the Forbidden City. The latter presented the artist with rare imperial porcelains and at the same time made him head of the Ching Chung Monastery. Under Manchu rule, to be head of that institution was the highest honour one in the profession could attain. Mr. Mei Lan-fang was also permitted to retain his title, "Foremost of the Pear Orchard," which designation implies that he was the first actor of the land; for, during the T'ang dynasty, under Ming Huang, the Imperial Troupe called themselves "Disciples of the Pear Orchard," because they performed in a palace surrounded by pear-trees.

A first impression of Mr. Mei Lan-fang may be quoted here from the *North-China Daily News*:

> "The great Mei, who does not prolong our wait as do most well-known, near-great men, enters so noiselessly that he is bowing to the visitor before the latter has time to regain enough composure to return the courtesy. Charmingly reserved is the actor. . . . But in those very silences and sincere evasions of anything that savours of personal praise lies a wealth of subtle power. . . .

The Actor in His Garden—Typical Pool and Rockery

The Actor in His Library of Chinese Books

"The simplicity of his dress further enhances his fair complexion and harmonizes with his silences; but his eyes light with animation as he listens with a warmth and sympathy that are, in themselves, a fine art. . . . His hands are remarkably graceful, even when not in motion. All the while, his intimate friends continue to give detailed accounts of his glories. . . . The actor seems to withdraw from the circle; there is no physical movement on his part, merely a mental shrinking from praise and publicity."[1]

Modest in life, brilliant on the stage, this most beloved of actors gives to the public his all. Yet people demand so much of his time that Mr. Mei spends days at social affairs when he might well be devoting himself to research or merely enjoying the priceless luxury of privacy. The very public which helps to make an artist does not hesitate, in its well-meant but thoughtless admiration, to snatch away the leisure necessary for full artistic achievement. That Mr. Mei, in spite of merciless social obligations, has accomplished as much as he has, is, indeed, nothing short of miraculous.

North-China Daily News, Shanghai, Nov. 13, 1926.

THE FEMALE IMPERSONATOR OF
THE CHINESE STAGE

NOTE

The term "female impersonator" as widely accepted by English-speaking peoples does not fully convey the meaning of the Chinese character *tan*. The latter is a designation for actors who specialize in feminine rôles on the Chinese stage. It is not realistic impersonation of the opposite sex that is sought but a highly conventionalized artistry. The spectator sees the idealized charms of a woman and experiences the æsthetic pleasure that comes of an actor's creating a picture that is as far removed as possible from all personal elements. When "female impersonator" is used in this book, it is employed in this special sense.

CHAPTER III
THE FEMALE IMPERSONATOR OF THE CHINESE STAGE

SOME time ago the title of the widely read book *The Changing Chinese* became a familiar catchword. Indeed, the people of this vast republic have been experimenting with new things, and momentous and far-reaching results have been produced. Change, transition, the period of political tutelage — these words and others attempt to picture the ferment which is now taking place in this nation of gigantic surprises. But, in the midst of sweeping change, firmly entrenched and ancient institutions, such as the guilds, may be found.

The institution of the *tan*, or female impersonator, still holds its own. The occident, which may have allowed the memory of Shakespeare's heroines who were portrayed by youths to grow dim, may ask, "Why do men portray feminine rôles?" A brief reply follows:

The emperor Ch'ien Lung in the eighteenth century issued an edict forbidding the appearance of women on the stage. This act not only necessitated the employment of handsome youths to portray feminine rôles, but it also gave the latter a firm foothold in the profession, which they continue to maintain to-day. In this connection, it may be interesting to quote from an article, "The Chinese Actress," in *Asia*, as follows:

"Although female entertainers continued down through the Sung (960-1126), it was not until the Yüan period (1280-1368) that women attained what we now consider the professional status of an actress. Thereafter, she made rapid progress in the field, until, by imperial edict, she was temporarily suppressed, only to reappear in Tientsin during the reign of Kuang Hsü (1875-1908). It was after the founding of the Republic, however, that theatres for all-female companies were established in Peking, Shanghai, Tientsin, and Canton, and that actresses gained a firm position with the public."[1]

"Gained a firm position" must be read with some qualification, for men are so well entrenched that actresses mimic, in some cases to the last detail, the style of the man who stands at the top of his peculiar school of acting and singing. The strange situation has arisen wherein a woman has imitated the vocal style of a man who himself had originally created a falsetto for the purpose of imitating, in a highly conventionalized manner, the voice of a real woman. At the present writing, there is in Peking a widely advertised actress who has gained her prestige by adopting two-thirds of a famous actor's name, by presenting his popular plays, and by making her voice approximate as closely as possible that of her male model.

In the not distant past men acted every rôle in a drama; but when all-female troupes came into existence, women portrayed not only the heroine but also the bearded general, the youthful scholar, and other male characters. But what of mixed companies, in which each sex acts the rôle natural to him? Although such companies are not unusual in Shanghai to-day, yet only a few years ago there was but one large playhouse in which members of both sexes appeared. While this theatre drew the patronage of some of the public, not a few men, who were modern-minded in every other respect, would refer to the playhouse with severe criticism. When Peking actors of note fill a short contract in Shanghai, the actresses of the theatre are given a vacation. A leading actor in Peking to-day would consider it a fatal blow to his reputation

---

[1] *Asia*, Dec., 1927.

if he were to appear with artists of the opposite sex. In private and benefit performances, however, actors and actresses may appear in separate plays during an evening.

China does not stand alone in the practice of men impersonating women on the stage. A student of Japanese drama must acquaint himself with the work of the *onnagata*, or the youth who acts feminine rôles. One still hears of former Italian male sopranos who essayed the parts of operatic heroines.

There are to-day in Peking two training schools for boy-actors, just as there were in London in Shakespeare's day. To quote from Volume II of *Shakespeare's England*:

> "In addition to these adult players there were two companies of 'children,' or boy-actors. . . . The formation of these companies was obviously a development of the stage convention by which in Shakespeare's day the parts of women were played by boys."[1]

Before considering the vocal technique of the *tan* and the conventional character types, let us imagine we are now in a Peking theatre attending a performance by Mr. Mei Lan-fang. It is a Saturday night in the Kaiming Theatre, which is crowded to the doors. Short plays of varying interest have been shown since early in the evening. It is well towards 11 p.m. when the lights blaze on the embroidered hangings of the stage, where, to the deafening clapping of hands and the shouting of *hao* (good), the artist, a vision of colour, makes his appearance. In this much-liked playlet, Mr. Mei impersonates Yang Kuei-fei, the favourite of the emperor Ming Huang (A.D. 713-755). The very slender story apparently serves as a framework for the pantomime, the dances, and the dreamy, wine-laden songs, which no one can present with the consummate artistry of Mei.

---

[1] *Shakespeare's England*, Vol. II, pp. 244-246.

The senses, fully gratified, do not know that the plot is insignificant, but they revel in the colour, action, and incomparable postures. Darkly jealous, and her pride wounded because the emperor was spending the night with her rival, Kuei-fei drains one bumper of strong wine after another until she reels about the stage in a series of gracefully tottering dances. There are also gymnastic feats, which require perfect muscular control, all effort being concealed by a training that has begun in childhood. The inimitable flourish of a sleeve, the quivering of a gold fan, the flash of eyes heavy with wine, half-closed with passion — these are but some of the fine touches an artist may add to a play.

Apart from the rôles for old women and *comédiennes*, female stage characters use a falsetto style, which, admittedly artificial, gains its appeal through intricate and conventionalized standards. Such singing and recitation may sound shrill and unmusical to most foreign ears. The *hsiao-shêng*, or rôle for a youth, is the only male stage character also using the falsetto.

From an article which appeared in the *China Journal* will be quoted passages which illustrate the manner in which Chinese writers differentiate the feminine stage types. While one Chinese investigator at least disagrees with this mode of classification, he has not yet offered an improved system, and when he does it is hoped he will soon publish it. Until this is done, it is only reasonable to use the widely accepted classification, which follows:

There are no less than six types of *tan* on the Chinese stage, and some native writers add to that number by making even more minute sub-divisions. The term *tan* covers, in general, the whole class of impersonators, which is sub-divided into the six following groups:

1. *Chêng-tan*, or *ch'ing-i* (正旦 或 青衣)
2. *Hua-tan* (花旦)
3. *Kuei-mên-tan* (閨門旦)
4. *Ts'ai-tan* (彩旦)
5. *Lao-tan* (老旦)
6. *Wu-tan* (武旦)

Mr. Mei Lan-fang as Mu Kuei-ying, a Military Type

The distinctions between these six classes are both numerous and detailed; but mention of the types and the manner of acting is a convenient means of entering this intricate subject.

The *chêng-tan*, more popularly known as the *ch'ing-i*, is the type representing the good matron, the faithful wife, or the filial daughter. In this type, singing is greatly stressed, and no fighting and gymnastics are required: indeed, when the characters 青衣 (*ch'ing-i*) appear on a theatre programme over the name of an actor, the audience settle comfortably in their seats and are prepared to enjoy several arias of the highest order, and woe to the reputation of the actor who proves vocally inferior.

The *hua-tan*, usually a younger woman than the *ch'ing-i*, may be a demi-mondaine or maidservant. Generally speaking, the *ch'ing-i* is the type for a good woman, and singing, especially the plaintive kind, is dominant; while the *hua-tan* is often the rôle for a woman of questionable morals, great emphasis being placed on the acting. The *hua-tan*, in order to be true to conventional requirement, should wear tiny, artificial feet.

Of the remaining four types, the *kuei-mên-tan* is an unmarried girl; while the *wu-tan*, of which the " sword and horse " *tan* is a type, is a military maiden. One of the most realistic types is the *lao-tan*, the rôle for an aged woman, often a mother. Another division is the *ts'ai-tan*, who delineates a wicked woman, an evilly inclined female servant, or the ever-present matchmaker.

These types are rigidly bound by certain conventional requirements of demeanour and action. The good woman, or *ch'ing-i*, is retiring, gracious, and refined. The *hua-tan* is bold and full of charm and seduction. The maidenly type, or *kuei-mên-tan*, is elegant, attractive, and graceful. The *ts'ai-tan*, while sometimes beautiful and graceful, is trifling by nature and often mean. The *wu-tan*, or military type, is both good to look upon and heroic; and the type for an old woman, or *lao-tan*, is usually gentle.

Characteristic actions often give a clue to the type. The *ch'ing-i* is most properly behaved: in her action there is not a vestige of seduction. Her footsteps are even and carefully taken; and, while walking, the feet are kept close to the ground. The hands, always in a graceful and dignified position, are often crossed. On entering or withdrawing, the head is inclined slightly forward; on leaving the stage, the right sleeve is often elevated.

With due allowance for her youth, the *kuei-mên-tan*, or maidenly type, is somewhat like the *ch'ing-i* in correct behaviour.

Most seductive and charming are the ways of the demi-mondaine, or *hua-tan* type, as she sways with airy grace to the stage on her false " golden lilies," her left hand on her waist and her right holding a silk handkerchief. Her every movement vibrates with life, from the suggestive and devastating glance of her eyes to the coy turn of her head. Unlike the foregoing types, she may perform gymnastic and military action. In order to charm the spectator to the very last, she, on leaving the stage, turns her head alluringly toward the audience with a smile that begins at the eyes and spreads down over the luscious curves of her cheeks and lips, or she may lift her right foot to reveal a flash of her red satin trousers.

The *ts'ai-tan*, in point of liveliness, is akin to the *hua-tan*. She is comic, lowly, and detestable. Her long strides are full of action; her eyes roll in diabolical mischievousness. And to prove that she is not a lady, she walks with crooked legs! On entering or going off, she makes a strange movement or smiles intriguingly at the audience.

As has already been mentioned, the type for an old woman, or *lao-tan*, is the most realistic. With lowered head and stooped shoulders she totters across the stage. A long staff is her indispensable support. She is gentle and motherly. Her eyes mirror the tired expression of old age.

In spite of the aforementioned conventions and many more which restrict an actor, a great artist may, by his genius, overcome the rigid requirements,

An Operatic Type in the Dress of a Poverty-Stricken Woman

offering not only a true picture of life, but often the very essence of realism, denuded of the commonplace.[1]

Here it is possible to make only brief reference to the peculiar art and some of the many dramas of the female impersonator. It is hoped that students of oriental and of world drama will make a special study of this most interesting phase of the Chinese theatre.

[1] *China Journal*, Vol. V, No. 4, Oct., 1926, pp. 164-174.

MR. MEI'S CONTRIBUTIONS TO CHINESE DRAMA

CHAPTER IV
MR. MEI'S CONTRIBUTIONS TO CHINESE DRAMA

WITH the passing of one generation, a theatrical idol may be forgotten. Such a favourite, delighting a grateful world with his talent and his youth, creates nothing in his own field to keep alive his memory. He may have had no desire to do so; he may have been happier to take what life had to give and go on. Since Mr. Mei Lan-fang is the idol of idols and as such is invested with a certain legendary grandeur, those who are interested in his art rather than in the momentary pleasure of seeing him once or twice, may wish to know what the artist has done for the theatre.

Before considering some of the revivals and innovations made by the actor, it may be well to describe briefly a Chinese audience. A playwright certainly writes for his public, just as an actor acts for it; and any discussion of contributions to a certain period of drama would be incomplete without a study of the audience. Outstanding is the fact that the majority of Chinese spectators are unaccustomed to, and do not demand, a realistic representation of life, because they come to the theatre to escape the dull cares of routine. They come to hear songs, the clangour of earsplitting brass, to delight in a fiercely painted face and its loud, extravagant voice, to see the supernatural mingle freely with people of flesh and blood, to see the good rewarded and the wicked punished. They find pleasure, above all, in the art and the personality of the actor. Essentially they do not differ from seekers of diversion the world over, although what they enjoy may be centuries removed, say, from a realistic or psychoanalytical drama which may be seen on Broadway.

The audience, which, generally speaking, is unfamiliar with modern stage technique and carefully developed plots, does not expect them. The few students who have been abroad and have studied modern stagecraft are of little consequence to the booking office. The people come armed with facts from history, novel, and legend; they expect to see characters with whom they have been familiar from childhood; they wish to hear much, or the greater part, of the story sung in a highly conventionalized manner.

Except a few large theatres in Peking, where the high admission fee keeps away some of the rabble, the ordinary playhouse is a kind of large social hall, in which one may do as he pleases: chat, exchange courtesies with his neighbour, eat whatever may come to his fancy, bring the maidservants with the children, and so on. The apparent inattention, it should be said, usually takes place during the early part of the afternoon or evening when unimportant actors appear in playlets known to the audience for decades. But when the star comes on and additional lights blaze forth, every one turns expectant eyes on the actor, who, although he may appear in a play which is no better than those just presented by lesser artists, receives both applause and attention. The situation again makes it clear that in China an actor is the important attraction in the theatre.

The conventionalization of Peking drama places an artist in an awkward position. If he acts always in strict accordance with tradition, he may be accused by modernists of being a case of arrested development and incapable of producing anything new. If he attempts that which is off the beaten path of convention, he may be condemned for violating the requirements of

MR. MEI'S CONTRIBUTIONS TO CHINESE DRAMA 29

the old school, mainly because his ability is not equal to the demands made by tradition.

With such an audience and such conditions, Mr. Mei Lan-fang has had to cope. The actor has not only helped to revive some of the better plays along with their music, but he has been able to introduce into the old theatre a new type of feminine character which combines accepted traditional elements with details he himself has added as a result of his investigations of the theatrical art of the past.

Mr. Mei has rendered great service by helping to revive the older musical drama, known as the *k'un-ch'ü*, which flourished during the Yüan (1280-1368) and Ming (1368-1644) periods, but which almost disappeared from the professional stage during the late Manchu dynasty. The *k'un-ch'ü* drama, sung to the soft notes of the flute, was displaced by the now all-popular *p'i-huang* drama with its more strident *hu-ch'in*, or so-called Chinese violin, and loud brass instruments.

It is Mr. Mei's popularity that enables him to present, if he pleases, as many as two *k'un-ch'ü* plays on three evenings. Again, he may interpolate a *k'un* song in a work otherwise *p'i-huang*, as in *The Heavenly Maiden Scattering Flowers*, an operatic dance drama, in which he does his first dance singing with the *hu-ch'in* and his second dance to the flute, which leads the soft music of the *k'un-ch'ü* orchestra.

Of the many things associated with the old stage which were in danger of being discarded until Mr. Mei restored them, only two will be cited. Although the important stringed instruments, the *yüeh-ch'in*, or moon guitar, and the southern *yin-tzŭ*, had been left out of orchestras, the actor reinstated them to their rightful positions, with the result that they may be heard in all theatres. Very striking and peculiarly Chinese was the head-dress of blue kingfisher feathers, arranged on a circular frame of silver. Later actors preferred ornaments of glass and imitation pearl. Mr. Mei had only to wear in his dramas the blue head-dress, and he won such enthusiastic approval that other female impersonators followed suit.

The outstanding contributions Mr. Mei has made to drama are his ancient costume plays, which are imitated by actors throughout the length and the breadth of China, as well as by artists of Japan and dancers in America.

The most important features of these plays, which are collectively known as the Mei School, are the actor's contribution of song linked with the dance and the ancient costume, which are added to two distinctive elements of the old drama, the whole being harmoniously blended by the genius of the actor. To make clear the point: first, it should be said that in former days actors of feminine parts were noted either for the operatic rôles of virtuous women or for the histrionic parts of vivacious women; and each style was kept rigidly separate. Not only did Mr. Mei successfully combine the two existing styles, but he also added the ancient costumes and the dance linked with song. It should be noted that in the distant past, song and dance were combined; but, as time passed, the dancing disappeared, while the song remained. Happily, from the actor's study of old books, the combination of dance and song was restored.

As for dances which grace many of Mr. Mei's dramas and which are the delight of the foreign spectator, only a few will be mentioned: the streamer dance, in *The Heavenly Maiden Scattering Flowers*; the pheasant plume dance, in *The Patriotic Beauty Hsi Shih*; the sleeve dance, in *The Goddess Shang Yüan*; the flag dance, in the third act of the *Yang Kuei-fei* series; and so on. In many of these dances there is much posturing, as when the actor, having sung to the end of a measure, poses in an attitude which is typical of Chinese dramatic art.

As for the magnificent costumes, which have been created as the result of the artist's study of ancient feminine dress on old bronze cauldrons, bells, paintings, etc., it is difficult to say whether the artist lends charm to the gowns or vice versa. The two, at any rate, are inseparable. A Chinese woman who has followed the work of the actor for years has constantly remarked, "It is only Mr. Mei who can wear these garments so as to show off their greatest possibilities." Needless to say, the artist is careful to give the costumes of the different characters that individual stamp which characterizes his various interpretations.

While the dramas just considered are linked with the actor's name, mention should be made of the various plays from the famous love novel, *Hung Lou Mêng*. Mr. Mei has, from time to time, based dramas on episodes from this literary masterpiece.

The foregoing is but a brief consideration of the revivals and the contributions the actor has made to the Chinese theatre. He will soon establish a school for the study of the best Chinese dramatic art. It is plain that Mr. Mei Lan-fang is interested in the betterment of the theatre, as well as in creating dramas suited to his own personality and peculiar talent, thus further endearing himself to his public.

DRAMAS PRODUCED BY MR. MEI

In the following pages an attempt will be made to consider briefly some of the dramas which were produced by Mr. Mei alone or in collaboration and which display his artistry.

The Love of Têng Hsia-ku
(鄧霞姑)
1913

This is the first drama on a modern theme but patterned on old conventions that Mr. Mei Lan-fang has produced, its moral being a protest against the tyranny of the old family system, especially as it has to do with the marriage problem. The action of the story centres about a young girl who chooses her own lover and arranges her own engagement. After eloping with the youth and passing through untold hardship, she attains her ideal. The play, which contains many pictures of social conditions, has found much favour with the public.

The Imprisoned Lovers
(牢獄鴛鴦)

This play is also an attempt on the actor's part to present a social-problem drama, the central idea being the true love between man and maid. Love should be regulated by the rules of virtue. Mr. Mei impersonates the young girl, who, for the sake of love, endures all manner of suffering, and after spending much time in prison, at last finds an opportunity to explain to her lover the misunderstanding that had existed between them. The couple are happily reunited. This is an example of drama, sung in the old conventional style but depicting present social conditions.

Ch'ang O's Flight to the Moon
(嫦娥奔月)
1914

This play is an early operatic dance creation, based on an ancient fairy tale, which tells how Ch'ang O, the wife of Hou I, stole the pill of immortality and fled to the moon to become queen.

Tai-yü Burying the Blossoms
(黛玉葬花)
1915

Tai-yü Burying the Blossoms is a dramatized episode from the famous novel, *Hung Lou Mêng*, an account of which may be found in Chapter V.

A Strand of Flax
(一縷麻)

A Strand of Flax, one of Mr. Mei's dramas in the tragic vein, has for its theme a twofold purpose: first, the glorification of the virtue of Chinese

The Maidservant Ching-wên, as Impersonated by Mr. Mei

The Actor in the Male Attire of a Warrior in the Play *Mu-lan in the Army*

womanhood; second, the portrayal of life in an old conservative family. When the actor impersonates a youthful and virtuous maiden, he invariably moves his audience to tears.

A Beauty's Smile
(千金一笑)
1916

A Beauty's Smile, popularly known among Chinese as *Ching-wên Tearing the Fan*, also comes from the pages of the novel *Hung Lou Mêng* and is concerned with the ravishingly pretty maidservant, Ching-wên, who is enjoying a playful moment with her youthful master, Pao-yü. The scenes, graphically depicting life in the women's apartments of a large family, are unlike those of *Tai-yü Burying the Blossoms*. Mr. Mei Lan-fang's ability lies in his excellent interpretations of women of all stations of life, whether she be the high-born and tearful Tai-yü or the winsome and capricious maidservant Ching-wên.

The Heavenly Maiden Scattering Flowers
(天女散花)
1917

This play, perhaps the actor's most beloved operatic dance drama, is described in Chapter V.

Mu-lan in the Army
(木蘭從軍)
1918

Mu-lan was a maid of old who disguised herself as a youth in order to go to war instead of her aged and ill father. Hence the plot offers unusual situations when Mr. Mei Lan-fang, in the leading rôle, dons the clothes of a warrior.

MEI LAN-FANG

Ma Ku Offering Birthday Gifts
（麻姑獻壽）
1919

This is an ancient costume play, based on a Chinese fairy tale, in which the actor impersonates the fairy Ma Ku.

A Young Girl Kills a Serpent
（童女斬蛇）

This work is a social-problem play, which has for its object the destruction of certain deep-rooted superstitions. Mr. Mei Lan-fang takes the part of the youthful but courageous heroine.

Hung Hsien's Theft of the Box
（紅線盜盒）

The play *Hung Hsien's Theft of the Box*, which finds its theme in the records of heroic deeds in the T'ang dynasty (618-906), deals with a brave and high-minded maiden, Hung Hsien, who could travel through the air at an incredible speed, leaving no trace of her presence at her stopping places. How she intimidated a wicked feudal lord and brought him to lead a better life, and how she used her sword with almost supernatural dexterity make a breathless tale.

The Goddess Shang Yüan
（上元夫人）
1920

The Goddess Shang Yüan is an operatic dance drama, which is presented annually on the occasion of the Lantern Festival. The tale is concerned with Han Wu-ti, the renowned monarch of the Han dynasty (206 B.C. to A.D. 221), who sought the secret of immortality.

Mr. Mei Lan-fang as the White Damsel in a Play Based on the Legend of the White Snake

Hsi Shih, the Patriotic Beauty

Lien Ching-féng as She Appears in a Marine Battle

The Goddess of the River Lo

MR. MEI'S CONTRIBUTIONS TO CHINESE DRAMA 35

The King's Parting with His Favourite
(霸王別姬)

This historical tragedy vividly reveals the last moments of the mighty warrior, Hang Yü (*circa* 200 B.C.). His successive defeats and reluctant parting with his beautiful favourite, the Lady Yü, are unfolded in scenes of dramatic intensity. The sorrowful songs and a sword dance by the heroine are but two of the features which have won for the play one of the greatest ovations in the history of the Chinese theatre.

The Patriotic Beauty Hsi Shih
(西施)
1921

Hsi Shih is the beauty who, by her heroic sacrifice, has won an everlasting place in the hearts and imagination of her fellow-countrymen. The setting in the Spring and Autumn period (722-484 B.C.) is concerned with the struggle between the Wu-Yüeh kingdoms.

Beauty in a Fisherman's Net
(廉錦楓)
1922

Lien Ching-fêng is a filial daughter, who searches the depths of the [oc]ean for sea-cucumbers, an indispensable ingredient for her mother's medicine. [Th]ere is an interesting marine battle in which the girl slays a gigantic bivalve [tak]ing from the creature a huge pearl.

The Goddess of the River Lo
(洛神)

This play, rich in literary quality, is an operatic dance drama. The essay *Lo Shên Fu*, which is the basis of the work, was written by Ts'ao Chih, the son of the Ts'ao Ts'ao of Three Kingdoms' fame (221-265). Following the original both in letter and in spirit, the drama shows a river goddess, who in reality is the shade of the writer's parted beloved. In a dream, Ts'ao Chih beholds the divine apparition on the banks of the River Lo dancing, beckoning, and revealing her love for him. The play is done in a tragic vein, and is, on the whole, as the Chinese puts it, " light as air, eluding all verbal description." The entire spirit of the delicate essay lives in Mr. Mei's dancing and singing; hence many critics consider the production the best of the literary-operatic type.

Yang Kuei-fei
（太真外傳）
1925

Yang Kuei-fei, also known as *T'ai Ch'ên Wai Chuan*, is an historical drama in four acts, which brings to life the most artful of China's four great beauties, Yang Kuei-fei, favourite of the licentious monarch, T'ang Ming Huang. It required two years of preparation on the part of Mr. Mei and his associates to complete the series.

Yang Kuei-fei, the Most Artful of China's Four Greatest Beauties, as Portrayed by Mr. Mei

REPRESENTATIVE DRAMAS OF MR. MEI

CHAPTER V
REPRESENTATIVE DRAMAS OF MR. MEI

LIKE the great singers of the Metropolitan Opera House, foremost Chinese actors in Peking appear about three times a week. Mr. Mei Lan-fang usually offers his plays at the week-end, alternating between the Kaiming and Chungho theatres. When filling an engagement in Shanghai, however, which he visits every two years or less, the actor appears on forty successive evenings and on Sunday afternoons.

Because, on each night in a Chinese playhouse, it is the custom to present a new programme, consisting of six to ten short dramas, it is clear that the star, whose play comes at the end of the long evening, must have a large and varied repertoire. Mr. Mei has at his command a few hundred plays. During the period of February 16 to April 7, 1929, in Peking, only two plays were repeated. One was produced three times, for it dealt with the Lantern Festival; the other was shown twice—once on the professional stage and once as a benefit performance. On the other hand, the actor has appeared in two short dramas on the same evening.

Moving from one theatre to another to act for a few days presents many practical problems, because in Peking no two modern-style playhouses are of the same dimensions, and the acoustical quality of the building may, by a noticeable degree, increase or decrease the volume of the voice.

While the Chinese public have at least one preference in common, that is, their love for song, yet, in other matters their divergence of taste makes many demands on the actor who would hold his public for any length of time. Quality and variety must mark his acting. One group of the public insists on the adherence to old classic convention with painstaking care; another insists on modified works, which, while having more action and certain slight changes, do not lose sight of the old conventions; a third ultra-modern group champions spoken drama, after the manner of the plays of America and Europe, and would be glad to have the old operatic drama done away with. From this state of affairs, it is clear that a Chinese actor has much with which to occupy his mind if he is to please most of the audience much of the time!

One of the gifts of Mr. Mei Lan-fang is that he knows his public and the times. Although he began his modest career at the early age of eleven, he enhanced his native ability by intensive study of all the technical and conventional material available in his field. Beginning with the *ch'ing-i*, or conventional type for a sedate and virtuous woman, for which the best of singing is demanded, the actor gradually acquired another style, that of the *hua-tan*, or the type for a vivacious woman or mischievous maidservant, which requires skilful acting rather than singing. Mr. Mei also studied the ways of real women and added to his interpretations an individuality entirely his own.

In the early years of the Republic, when revolution affected not only the political but the artistic and mental life of the nation as well, Mr. Mei introduced the ancient costume drama. Other distinctive types of plays to be found in the actor's repertoire are those containing rôles for military maidens, for heroines who sing to the accompaniment of the flute, and for the immortal beauties from the love novel *Hung Lou Mêng*.

First will be considered a *ch'ing-i*, or operatic rôle, a supreme test of an actor's mettle, because the exacting nature of the requirements precludes all possibility of becoming a star except for those who are truly gifted and who labour assiduously to make the most of their natural talent.

The long drama *Yu Chou Fêng*, which may be retitled in English *The Fateful Sword*, and which has been revived in its length of forty scenes by Mr. Mei, contains the famous " mad scene," which is often sung as a separate playlet. Singing and acting of a most difficult nature characterize the scene in question. Here are stressed the fact that the Chinese woman of old thought it a breach of virtue to wed the second time and the fact that she would struggle to protect what she believed her chastity.

From the long drama, only the episodes dealing with Chao Nü's feigning madness will be chosen to illustrate the art of an impersonator in a *ch'ing-i*, or operatic rôle. Mr. Mei Lan-fang portrays the heroine, Chao Nü, who, after her marriage to K'uang Fu and the decline of the K'uang family, had no choice except to return to her unscrupulous father, Chao Kao. The latter was a favourite of the lascivious Ch'in Êrh Shih, the son of the renowned builder of the Great Wall, Ch'in Shih Huang-ti (221-209 B.C.).

When Êrh Shih visits Chao Kao and espies the latter's pretty daughter, he offers to receive the young woman into his palace. While the father is eager to effect so profitable a match, the daughter, on the other hand, holds firmly to the old-time belief that a woman should remain true to her husband. She is at her wit's end as to how to ward off her insistent parent, when the dumb maidservant motions that she should feign madness.

Having disarranged her clothing and allowed her hair to become dishevelled, Chao Nü sings the full, high notes which are descriptive of her state of mind. When she sinks on the floor, the action is enhanced by the graceful flourish of her sleeves, which are wrapped tightly about her wrists. In Peking drama, beauty of action may be added to plain movement in order to please the eye. Chao Kao is in the end convinced of his daughter's insanity when she pursues him, calling him her son and later making amorous advances.

But the heroine, who is determined to maintain what in her eyes is her chastity, has yet to prove to the emperor that she is insane. Preceded by her father, she swaggers like a courtier to the Dragon Throne. Gestures and flourishes of the sleeves heighten the dramatic effect as she reviles the emperor. She remains defiant even when her father sings, " Stop, it will cost you your head ! " Leaning on the shoulder of her faithful maidservant, Chao Nü laughs wildly into the faces of the four guards who point their gleaming weapons at her defenceless body. Believing the beauty truly mad, Êrh Shih orders her home.

In this part of the play may be seen the following characteristics of Peking drama : (1) The great stress placed on a woman's protecting her virtue — a theme which occurs in innumerable plays; (2) singing — to express the emotions when they have been raised to a certain pitch; (3) the flourish of sleeves — to enhance an ordinary action or any other graceful movement to afford the eyes additional pleasure.

The acting of Chao Nü may be realistic in suggestion only, because grace must be included in the general action. Singing, too, heightens the effect. Thus it is that Mr. Mei Lan-fang is ideal in the part. He can make one feel keenly the helplessness of a young woman who struggles against what seems to be overwhelming odds. At the same time, the spectator may enjoy the conventional grace of action, coupled with singing — features which are distinctive characteristics of the Peking School.

The *hua-tan*, or type for a vivacious woman, which stresses acting, was exemplified in the playlet of Chapter III by the rôle of Yang Kuei-fei, the beauty who, under the influence of wine, which she had taken to drown her jealousy, did a series of tottering dances. Another well-defined *hua-tan* character which is frequently seen is that restless bit of sprightliness, the mischievous maidservant. She comes on the stage, her face bright with a smile, while her fingers never rest from toying with her sash or her handkerchief. Her tight-fitting costume, usually consisting of a long vest tied at the waist with a sash, short sleeves, and trousers, allows her the freedom of movement denied the sedate and properly behaved *ch'ing-i*, who wears knee-length coats, from which her full sleeves hang almost to the ground. In an old drama from the Yüan dynasty, Mr. Mei impersonates the naughty maidservant Ch'un Hsiang, who plays pranks on her aged teacher; again, he may impersonate an equally active maidservant who makes possible the union of two youthful lovers.

While Mr. Mei continues to act plays which are strictly operatic or histrionic, he has ingeniously combined the two to create a more versatile type, which he has further enhanced by adding the dance and ancient costume. The result is the dazzling figure known as the ancient costume impersonator, who displays to excellent advantage the incomparable grace that is Mei's. It is this type of drama that appeals to the average foreigner.

Of this school of plays, the drama that is without doubt linked most closely with Mei, both in name and in a pictorial sense, is *T'ien Nü San Hua*, or *The Heavenly Maiden Scattering Flowers*, because the likeness of the actor, attired in the flowing garments of the T'ien Nü in an attitude of prayer, may be seen on silver plaques, porcelain, tapestry, glass, photographs, etc. The story of this drama, Buddhistic in conception, is concerned with Tathagata, the Buddhistic world saviour, who sent the Heavenly Maiden to dance and to scatter flowers when the devout Wei-mo-ch'i discoursed on the laws and the sutras to his disciples. To the sleeves of those who had overcome all carnal desire, the petals did not cling, but to the sleeves of those who still loved the world, the petals adhered tenaciously. On the latter, Wei-mo-ch'i would smile, saying, "You have not yet cut yourselves off from the world." From the foregoing incident is taken the theme and title of the play.

In the opening scene appear a bewildering array of Buddhistic dignitaries, among them being the four "cloud-sprites," the eighteen lo-hans, the Bodhisattva Manjusri, Tathagata, and others. Tathagata sings and declaims passages rich in Buddhistic teaching and then recites as follows: "I am he of the Western Heaven, Sakyamuni. To-day, since Wei-mo-ch'i is ill, I wish to order my followers to inquire after the good man's condition. . . . Manjusri!" Accordingly, Manjusri and other deities proceed to the earth.

The next scene discloses eight female attendants, two of whom carry tasselled standards, and two, long-handled fans. With this impressive retinue as a background, Mr. Mei Lan-fang makes his triumphal entrance as the Heavenly Maiden. The coat, usually of a brilliant, imperial yellow, the skirt, of a dazzling silver white, and the high picturesque coiffure make a handsome ensemble. The T'ien Nü waves a duster of horse-hair, an emblem of celestial beings, recluses, monks, etc.

After singing, the Heavenly Maiden proceeds, in the fashion peculiar to the Chinese stage, to recite: "I am T'ien Nü. I have received my commission from the Heavenly Father, who has ordered me to care for the flowers in the Kingdom of Fragrance. . . . When the disciples discourse on the sutras and the law, I scatter down flower petals to test their spiritual attainment."

Having received the celestial command to proceed to the abode of Wei-mo-ch'i, the maiden sings as she floats through the clouds. The present scene, called *The Dance in the Clouds*, is set to music, accompanied by the *hu-ch'in*, or so-called Chinese violin. While waving the silken streamers, T'ien Nü moves gracefully from side to side and stoops with that delicate refinement which is typical of Chinese terpsichorean art. As the song increases in tempo, the streamers are waved about until they create a vision of fluttering colour. In the finale the Heavenly Maiden kneels in a posture of prayer that is famous throughout the length and breadth of the country.

A vivid and mundane contrast to the ethereal scene just completed is the lively conversation that takes place between four youthful monks. One of them, who had been presented to the monastery when he was still an infant, argued against the others, who pointed out the merits of the religion.

In the meantime, Manjusri and his companions have arrived and inquired after Wei-mo-ch'i's health.

Mr. Mei Lan-fang as the Heavenly Maiden in an Attitude of Prayer which Is Famous in All China

Chen Miao-ch'ang, the Heroine of *The Jade Hairpin*

REPRESENTATIVE DRAMAS OF MR. MEI

The last scene discloses T'ien Nü on a cloud-terrace, where she sings a poem in praise of flowers. The long aria, which is accompanied by a dance, is an example of old *k'un-ch'ü*, a style characterized by the quiet notes of the flute. Mr. Mei has for some years been active in reviving public interest in the *k'un-ch'ü*; and, in order to do so, he often interpolates a *k'un* song in modern plays or presents a drama sung entirely in that manner.

The dance, done with a female attendant, is accompanied by the exquisitely soft notes of the flute and the *shêng*, the latter being a kind of ancient reed-organ. The music is a perfect setting for the Heavenly Maiden as she postures with long silken streamers and scatters flowers. Thus, when Wei-mo-ch'i bids his divine visitors farewell, the play ends in a veritable riot of colour.

The foregoing drama, with its dances, which are done to the accompaniment of song, and which are characterized by the equal stressing of acting and singing, is typical of the school Mr. Mei Lan-fang has created. The striking costumes and coiffures are also distinctive features of this group of plays.

An older style of play known as the *k'un-ch'ü*, and sung to the accompaniment of an orchestra in which the notes of the flute dominate, is *Yü Tsan Chi*, or *The Jade Hairpin*. The pretty nun, Chen Miao-ch'ang, because of the unsettled conditions in the country, lives with her aunt, who is the abbess of a monastery. The elder woman's nephew, Pan Pi-chêng, who is visiting her, has also made the monastery his temporary living quarters.

On a moonlight night the lovers carry on a flirtation by playing the *ch'in* and singing. The heroine proceeds to move her fingers with delicate grace over the strings of the instrument. Meanwhile, the youth purposely brushes against Miao-ch'ang, who, while pretending to be highly indignant, confesses to the audience in an aside, "And think you I have no desire for love?" Although her eyes are full of affection, the girl withdraws, closing the door. The following question asked by the heroine is typical of an old-fashioned maiden.

"With the brilliant moon shining on my lonely bed-curtains, who knows how many tears I shed?"

Pan is afflicted with love on the one hand and with a cold caused by the night air on the other. His mischievous manservant, Chin An, hints broadly at his master's infatuation. When the abbess and the girl come to inquire after Pan, the latter, as soon as he gazes upon the pretty nun, experiences immediate recovery!

On another evening, the youth tiptoes to the girl's room and pilfers from under her arm a poem in which she reveals her love. When Miao-ch'ang awakens and threatens to call her aunt, Pan triumphantly flaunts the poem, which he in turn threatens to show her aunt. He smiles, saying, "You, a nun, ought not to compose a poem to tempt a good youth like me!" To this, the girl cleverly retorts that she has written a Buddhist essay! When Pan playfully questions the truth of her statement, the lovers sing that their love will endure for ever.

The servant, Chin An, enters in the chilly dawn. After attracting the attention of the lovers by meowing like a cat, he demands forfeits of each before he will promise to keep their secret. When they are alone, Pan assures the sceptical servant, not without a touch of savage vehemence, that he has had nothing beyond a cup of tea in the charming young woman's room.

Another conventional type which Mr. Mei acts is the *wu-tan*, or military impersonator, who often is a warrioress or a woman skilled in gymnastics. *Hung-i Kuan,* or *Rainbow Pass,* which holds for the Chinese public a perennial charm, is a drama that has for its heroine a widow who goes forth to battle in order to avenge her husband's death.

The story follows:

Towards the end of the seventh century China was ground under the heels of contending armies of war-lords, from whom gradually arose powerful leaders. These forced most of the country to bow to their yoke; but they failed to conquer Rainbow Pass, which was guarded by the valiant Hsin Wên-li. When all efforts failed, the expert bowman, Wang Pai-tang, was sent to take the impregnable stronghold. Wang let fly the fatal shaft which ended Hsin's life. The pretty and youthful widow of the deceased mourned for her mate, swearing that she would slice the murderer bit by bit.

The widow, Tung-fang, who was a courageous fighter, adept horsewoman, and expert at wielding weapons, attacked the enemy forces with such spirit that the latter were in danger of being routed.

When the victorious woman met Wang Pai-tang face to face, the armies held their breath, because they well knew that one of the two would lie in the dust before the other left the field.

"Why did you kill my husband?" demanded Tung-fang, her hand firmly gripping her spear. As they came to close quarters and the woman caught a first glimpse of her enemy's handsome face, she became madly infatuated. Here certain well-defined characteristics of Chinese drama are to be seen. The widow, impersonated by Mr. Mei Lan-fang, raises her spear to strike Wang Pai-tang, who usually is portrayed by Mr. Chiang Miao-hsiang. Although it is understood that the two opponents are engaged in deadly combat, the actors, while displaying their gymnastic skill, also add much grace to every movement in order to form rhythmic pictures. The music and the songs serve to heighten the effect; each time the end of a vocal measure is reached, the man and the woman come to a complete pause, to create a tableau which describes Tung-fang's flirtation with her handsome enemy. Wang rejects her advances with a vivid "Peh!" After several songs and much posturing and graceful movements, which are supposed to mark the passing of the fray, the man defeats his fair opponent. She, however, resourceful to the last, has Wang taken prisoner by her men.

The foregoing, which is the first part of the drama, illustrates the action of a *wu-tan*.

Apart from the celestial and royal maidens created by Mr. Mei Lan-fang, the actor has produced another group of plays with which both the Chinese and some foreigners link his name. The dramas in question are those based on the literary masterpiece, of which Dr. Herbert A. Giles says in his book, *A History of Chinese Literature*: "The *Hung Lou Mêng*, conveniently but erroneously known as *The Dream of the Red Chamber*, is the work referred to already as touching the highest point of development reached by the Chinese novel. It was probably composed during the latter half of the seventeenth century. The name of its author is unknown. . . . No fewer than four hundred personages of more or less importance are introduced first and last into the story, the plot of which is worked out with a completeness worthy of Fielding, while the delineation of character—of so many characters—recalls the best efforts of the greatest novelists of the West."[1]

Of the dramas based on the *Hung Lou Mêng*, two will be considered: an early and still popular work in which Mr. Mei impersonates Tai-yü, an aristocratic beauty of strange but exquisite moods; and a recent production in which the actor plays the part of Hsi-jên, a vivacious maidservant.

Tai-yü Burying the Blossoms, produced in 1915, belongs to the ancient costume group. While there is no dancing, yet there are the graceful postures Tai-yü assumes while burying flowers.

The story in brief follows:

Tai-yü, whose parents have died, is sent to live with her wealthy grandmother. Being a creature of moods, she sees in the faded, bruised, and neglected petals a picture of herself, lonely, motherless, and destined to an early death. In a corner of the secluded garden she has had a mound built where she can take her hoe and bury the petals.

Giles, Herbert A., *A History of Chinese Literature*, p. 355.

Spring has come once more. On being told by her maidservant that the women of the great household have gone off to worship, the girl, who feels her sorrows keenly, turns her thoughts to the fallen petals.

Torn between jealousy and doubt as to whether her handsome cousin, Pao-yü, really loves her, Tai-yü proceeds toward the burial mound of flowers. While singing, she takes a broom and gently sweeps the petals into a heap. She places the withered flowers in a tiny bag, fastened to the pruning-hook that rests on her shoulder. After explaining and arguing away a small difference that has existed between them, the lovers feel more devoted than ever.

The tone-descriptions played by the stringed instruments are commendable efforts in the direction of a much-needed increase in variety in the music of Peking drama. Mr. Mei himself considers that, of all the heroines of ancient costume drama, Tai-yü demands the most exacting expression. Indeed, it is no easy task to re-create the immortal Tai-yü, a creature at once learned, witty, and given to moods, but on the whole a good companion to her much-spoiled cousin, Pao-yü.

The most recent drama of the *Hung Lou Mêng* group, *Charming Hsi-jên*, is distinctive in that it may, in a sense, be considered an example of transitional drama. While there are a goodly number of songs, yet there is also a noticeable increase in the number of spoken lines. Furthermore, many of the movements, while in general adhering to conventional requirement, are marked by an easy natural grace.

The increase in spoken lines points towards the spoken drama. While some modernized and foreign-educated Chinese are producing spoken plays written after the realistic style of the West, they have not yet won public favour. The song is still demanded. Thus it is that the audience may learn to appreciate the spoken drama if the number of spoken passages in the old operatic drama is increased.

In this gigantic task Mr. Mei can accomplish much; for, as may be seen in the discussion of the play to follow, the actor can invest his every action with such charm that any changes he may introduce will have a favourable opportunity of being received by his sympathetic audiences. This, however, is a side issue, for the main consideration here is the art of the actor. It has merely been pointed out that the Chinese drama is changing; that there is now in progress a period of transition.

Some lovers of the old may object to the introduction of new elements; but it should be made clear that Mr. Mei can act pure classical drama, that he is a master of the ancient costume type, and that he does exceptionally well in transitional dramas like the one which is about to be considered. It is when an artist indiscriminately mixes the old with the new that the situation is to be regretted. If an actor is master of the old and the transitional, and is able to interpret each school in its own purity, then he is more than justified in producing original plays combining the best elements of both types.

Such a drama is *Charming Hsi-jên*, in which Mr. Mei Lan-fang impersonates a vivacious, quarrelsome, stubborn, but attractive maidservant. The verbal battles of youth, with the patching up of wounded pride; the sudden anger, laughter, and tears of pretty Hsi-jên; the playful resistance of her handsome young master, Pao-yü—these form the basis of the play, many passages of which are quoted verbatim from Chapter XXI of the novel.

Hsi-jên, feeling slighted because Pao-yü has spent too much time with his cousin Tai-yü, wreaks her temper on the youth. The latter, on the other hand, proves to the irate beauty that in matters of temper he is every bit her match.

While singing, Hsi-jên sits embroidering, as is the case in Peking drama, with an imaginary needle and thread. The girl pretends that she is asleep. When Pao-yü enters and remarks that Hsi-jên is lazy, the latter at once opens her eyes and exclaims angrily, pouting as she tosses her long sleeve toward him, "Lazy! then I'll wait on your grandmother."

When Pao-yü in his turn pretends to sleep, Hsi-jên mischievously addresses an imaginary visitor, with the result that the youth gets up to see who has come. Hsi-jên gives him a triumphant smile.

Spectators find much amusement in these quarrels. Hsi-jên, who knows that she has been in the wrong, will not admit her fault to Pao-yü, although she confides to the audience in an aside that she is not in the right!

Pao-yü then falls asleep, having done his utmost to tease the enraged beauty. Then Hsi-jên, after arranging a coat over him, stretches herself wearily on the same lounge, also eventually falling asleep. The youth, on awaking, shows an equal solicitude by placing the coat on his fair companion, who ungratefully tosses the garment aside. With the passing of the night, Pao-yü, who has forgotten their difference, does his best to mend matters. The pair kneel as they become friends again.

While an attempt has been made to describe representative dramas as acted by Mr. Mei, yet one must see the plays in order to enjoy fully both their content and the art of the actor. Not only has Mr. Mei Lan-fang endeared himself to the hearts of his own countrymen, but he has been a source of unending pleasure to foreigners. It requires a rare artistry to entertain people of alien lands when there are the barriers of language and stage convention, which differ so widely from those found elsewhere. But as is true of art the world over, the incomparable grace and talent of the artist surmount all handicaps.

THE FOREIGN FRIENDS OF MR. MEI LAN-FANG

Miss Ruth St. Denis, Mr. Mei Lan-fang, and Mr. Ted Shawn in an Old Chinese Garden

Miss Ruth St. Denis, Mr. Mei Lan-fang, and Mr. Ted Shawn as They Appeared in a Joint Programme in Peking

CHAPTER VI
THE FOREIGN FRIENDS OF MR. MEI LAN-FANG

THE brilliant art and the gentle personality of Mr. Mei Lan-fang have won for him admirers and friends from the four corners of the earth. While it is a regrettable fact that few, if any, English newspaper cuttings concerning Mr. Mei have been kept on file, and that many of the names of his distinguished foreign visitors have been changed to Chinese phonetics, which make a correct decipherment an impossibility, yet it has been possible to recover some of the names of well-known visitors.

Dr. Rabindranath Tagore

When the great Tagore arrived in Peking, the first request he made of his host was that he be taken to see a drama by the Chinese actor. Messrs. Hsiung Hsi-ling, the first premier of the Republic, Lin Chang-min, and the late Liang Chi-chao arranged a meeting for the two well-known men.

On the day following, May 19, 1924, the Indian poet attended Mr. Mei's performance of *The Goddess of the River Lo*. At the conclusion of the operatic dance drama, Tagore remarked: " I have, in the past, not been favourably disposed towards the over-abundant use of scenery in the theatre. It has often occurred to me that if there were but a plain purple curtain and no other stage setting, the theme of the play and the beauty of the actors would so stand out as to render all property-encumbered drama insignificant. This was a fancy I had entertained for some years; but now that I have beheld the drama which has brought my fond fancy into reality, I confess that Mr. Mei Lan-fang has won my deep admiration. . . . As for the actor's stage presence and make-up, one would never doubt for a moment that he was a beautiful woman. . . . Suspense, variety, and other essential qualities were well handled, the finale being both charming and impressive to look upon."

The poet presented the actor with a fan.

Sir Claude Severn

In 1922 Mr. Mei arrived in Hongkong with a letter of introduction from the British Legation in Peking to the Acting Governor of Hongkong, Sir Claude Severn. The latter expressed his desire that the Chinese actor should tour England, adding that there was at the time a group of sixty people who were presenting in London old Chinese dramas.

The Crown Prince and Princess of Sweden

While visiting Japan, the Crown Prince of Sweden, Gustavus Adolphus, and the Crown Princess, Louise Alexandra, had heard so much of Mr. Mei's art that, on their arrival in Peking, they informed the Legation that they desired to attend a performance by the Chinese actor. Suitable arrangements were at once made for an informal gathering, the actor being requested to display his collection of rare fans, seals, jades, and other antiques.

It was on an evening of October in 1926; the corridors of the Mei gardens were hung with coloured gauze lanterns, and the pathways were banked with brilliant chrysanthemums. At 10 p.m. the two dramas *The Jade Hairpin* and *The King's Parting with His Favourite*, for which the Department of Foreign Affairs had prepared English programmes, were enacted.

The Crown Princess Louise Alexandra Seated Between the Crown Prince of Sweden, Gustavus Adolphus, and Mr. Mei

While Mr. Mei was applying his make-up, his guests remained in the reception room examining the display of antiques. The Crown Prince and Princess were delighted with an old yellow seal, weighing about two ounces. They had been seeking, for some days, just such a seal but had been unsuccessful. When the actor returned and discovered his royal guests' fascination for the tiny treasure, he took the seal in both his hands and with oriental courtesy proffered it to his visitors. The Crown Princess thanked her host, assuring him that on her return to her native land she would carefully treasure and hand down the seal to her sons as an heirloom and a perpetual reminder of the actor's hospitality.

The royal couple presented Mr. Mei with their autographed portraits.

During the interval between the two dramas, Messrs. Wang Shao-ching, Hsu Lan-yuan, Yang Pao-chung, Kao Lien-kuei, and Huo Wen-yuan formed a stringed quintet, playing *Willows Swaying Gold* and *The Mei Blossom Suite*.

Madame Galli-Curci

When the well-known diva visited Peking, she called on Mr. Mei Lan-fang, who had, on the night before, attended the singer's concert in the Hotel de Pekin. The operatic star was charmed by the dresses worn by the Chinese women present and took great delight in being photographed and filmed with the oriental beauties by her husband, Mr. Homer Samuels.

Mr. Rudolph Friml

When the composer of *Rose Marie* and other musical-comedy successes was in Peking with the round-the-world tourists on the *Empress of Australia*, he and some one hundred and twenty fellow-travellers attended the play the Chinese actor presents annually in commemoration of the Lantern Festival. It is said that Mr. Friml was enchanted with the groupings and dances.

Arrangements were made for composer and actor to meet in the latter's home. Mr. Friml, hoping that the artist would go to New York, explained to the latter something of the American taste and illustrated how the finales of his own musical productions were staged. The Chinese actor took great delight in hearing the New York composer play several of his own compositions, and asked his guest many questions concerning the theatrical situation in the eastern part of the United States. Since Mr. Friml has collaborated with such well-known producers as Mr. Ziegfeld, he was in a position to give much information of a direct and professional nature.

Mr. Frank Hedges

The American journalist and correspondent for the *Japan Advertiser*, Mr. Frank Hedges, passed through Shanghai on his way to India, whence he planned to return to the United States via Europe. As Mr. Mei at the time was filling an engagement in Shanghai, the two men met to discuss oriental drama. Apart from their agreeing that the old Chinese drama should be preserved intact, they discussed a variety of subjects.

Said Mr. Hedges: " Although I have lived in Japan for many years and have been a devotee of the theatre, yet it was when I attended your performances that I immediately understood the admirable qualities of Chinese theatrical art. . . . I should like to know whether you, Mr. Mei, have found helpful suggestions in Japanese drama."

To this Mr. Mei replied in his characteristic manner, giving full credit to a rival art, as follows: " The pantomime of Japanese drama is excellent; and in realistic scenery, Japan is far ahead of China. I may, in the future, make use of these good points on the Chinese stage."

Continued the journalist: " Although the Chinese may not be so far advanced as the Japanese in stage settings, yet, when the scenery is too imposing, audiences may devote their attention to them rather than to the actors. That, then, might easily prove a disadvantage."

The actor asked: "Since I have long entertained the wish to tour the chief cities of Europe and America in order to study the occidental stage, would you be so kind as to offer suggestions to that end?"

Mr. Hedges replied with much enthusiasm: "I will do my utmost to help you both in Washington and in New York City. . . . Your going to the United States, however, exposes you to one great danger." When the amazed actor asked what was the danger, his visitor smiled, saying: "It is simply my fear that when you see the drama of other countries, you will introduce foreign elements into Chinese theatrical art. Your stately dancing and exquisite singing are worthy representatives of the Chinese stage and would lose their purity if you were to allow foreign ideas to enter your field. You must guard against this danger."

Receiving the advice in a sympathetic mood, Mr. Mei said, by way of assurance: "Your words are very good. I will, indeed, keep them in my heart and strive to preserve the purity of my art."

Baron Okura

Mr. Mei Lan-fang's appearance in Japan had such far-reaching results in literary and artistic circles that the millionaire business magnate and director of the Imperial Theatre in Tokyo, Baron Kihachiro Okura, wrote to the Chinese actor that all classes of the Japanese public welcomed his plays, that Nipponese artists had new standards by which to judge their own work, and that the renowned actress Miss Kakuko Murata was about to present his play, *The Heavenly Maiden Scattering Flowers*.

The Foremost Japanese Artists, Miss Murata and Mr. Morita

The foremost dramatic artists of Japan who appear exclusively in the Imperial Theatre in Tokyo are Miss Murata and Mr. Morita. During his two engagements in that country, Mr. Mei appeared in the same theatre and contracted a warm friendship for his Japanese fellow-actors.

The actor Mr. Sadanji Ichikawa, recalling the Chinese actor's two visits to Japan, and remembering that Japanese actors had not yet toured China, organized a company to visit Peking. Unfortunately, civil war broke out, cutting off communication between Peking and Tientsin, with the result that the entire company was obliged to return to Japan.

Later, Mr. S. Yamamori, manager of the Tokyo Theatre, assembled a company of actors to tour China, securing the services of Miss Murata and Mr. Morita. The two Japanese celebrities and Mr. Mei Lan-fang offered representative works in the Kaiming Theatre.

At a tea given in honour of the visiting Japanese, Mr. Mei read an address of welcome, emphasizing that Chinese and Japanese art had much in common. He concluded as follows: "Thus, on this visit of our Japanese fellow-artists, we firmly believe that the Chinese public will understand true Japanese dramatic art and will derive from it great inspiration. To this end, we welcome our visiting friends and feel certain that their sojourn will be a glorious success." Applause followed, "loud like thunder."

Replying on behalf of the Japanese actors, Mr. Morita spoke as follows: "It was on Mr. Mei's first visit to our country that we, for the first time, really understood Chinese dramatic art. . . . At that time, the people of Japan were loud in their praise and servile in their imitation of European and American plays, as if, apart from these works, there were no other means to fame. Some of us persisted in the belief that oriental art possessed intrinsic values of its own and that it was altogether unnecessary to imitate the occident. We, therefore, have come to your great country for the express purpose of perpetuating the art of the East and of making the world recognize the true worth of the Chinese and the Japanese drama. A duty of such magnitude must be shouldered by the artistic circles of both countries. You, Mr. Mei, are the foremost actor of China and are recognized the world over as a protagonist of the best in oriental art. Feeling highly honoured to be your guests, we raise our cups to wish you long life."

Sir Robert Lorraine, Mr. Shen Kun-san, and Mr. Mei Lan-fang

On the third day, prominent Chinese were hosts at a tiffin given in the Hotel de Pekin. Mr. K. K. Feng, president of the Bank of China, delivered an address. By way of conclusion, Mr. Feng said: " While the international friendship of China and Japan leaves much to be desired, yet to-day this happy gathering, presided over by Messrs. Morita and Mei, is ample proof of a long-wished-for beginning of perfect understanding. Hereafter, the peoples of the two countries, as well as their diplomatic leaders, should use this happy event as a model for the improvement of international relationship."

The next morning, Mr. Mei went in person to the railway station in order to see his guests off. Miss Murata, Mr. Morita, and the entire party wore the Chinese garments that Mr. Mei Lan-fang had presented to them.

At the present writing, a few more names of well-known guests are available. The late General Leonard Wood and the former Secretary of the U. S. Navy Denby, have enjoyed plays by the actor. Mr. Somerset Maugham may be mentioned among the literary men who have visited Mr. Mei. Professional artists of the occident, such as Miss Ruth St. Denis and Mr. Ted Shawn, of the O'Denishawn Dancers, have passed many happy hours exchanging ideas with the Chinese actor.

By way of conclusion, it will bear repeating how deeply it is regretted that it has been necessary to omit the names of many interesting friends and callers because of the lack of records in English. For the many quotations, it is also hoped that the speakers will forgive any slight errors that may have been made, for the English was first translated into Chinese, and then, here, it has been translated once more into English. In the future, it is hoped that complete reports of such meetings, and especially those appearing in English publications, will be carefully filed.

MR. MEI LAN-FANG IN CHINESE EYES

CHAPTER VII
MR. MEI LAN-FANG IN CHINESE EYES

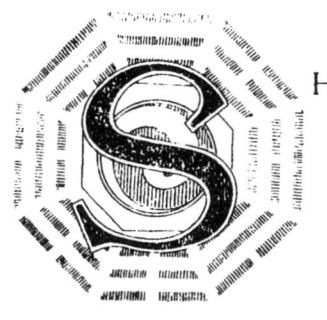SHOULD the casual foreign visitor attend a drama by Mr. Mei he would describe the acting of the artist as "graceful, exquisite, marvellous," etc.; or if he were a student of dramatics, he would often be startled by the perfection with which music, singing, gesture, and facial expression blend to create a harmonious impression. How much more would the outsider have to muse delightfully over while watching a performance, if he had in mind some of the phrases used by scholarly Chinese critics, such as follow: "His stage walk was graceful. His make-up, a little short of divine, emphasized his natural beauty. His voice, sweet like the oriole, was followed by the accompanist with such perfection that the combination literally exemplified the saying, 'For the full expression of its beauty, the peony relies on the contrast produced by its verdant leaves.'" Again, in regard to an operatic drama: "His voice, from the first note to the last, was clear like fragments of jade without blemish, while his tones of intense grief moved the audience deeply. . . . His enunciation was clear and mellow; his manners, the essence of refinement; thus it is no wonder that applause, endless like a rope of pearls, followed."

The foregoing translated passages are ordinary examples of the enthusiasm, the adoration, which the actor's artistry arouses in a scholarly critic. Although the present style of journalism, with its revolutionary turn towards simplicity, may discourage the poetical quality of the old-fashioned critic, yet one may still read in the newspapers and the magazines, on occasion, critiques full of the pictorial quality of the writing of the former generation.

An encomium, translated from the Chinese, is as follows:

"That Mr. Mei Lan-fang is heaven-sent and a most genial person is not for my humble pen to set forth, because for years the entire Middle Kingdom has never ceased to praise and to sigh over the sheer beauty of his art, the brilliance of his voice, and the exquisiteness of his appearance. In his praise, my friends and I have written endless numbers of poems, couplets, and essays. Apart from the many excellent qualities, of which the public are only too well aware, Mr. Mei possesses one that other actors cannot hope to equal, even in a small degree; namely, that quality on which the artist has built his reputation, the tireless energy he puts into every scene of his dramas.

"The artist devotes his entire mind, strength, and energy to any scene he presents, that his audiences may enjoy to the full his interpretations. Whenever one visits a playhouse, he may notice that the leading actor, completely satisfied with his past laurels, spares his effort and performs in an indifferent manner. Since in singing, declamation, and acting Mr. Mei is altogether unwilling to tolerate laziness in any form, he is, in this respect, head and shoulders above the entire galaxy of Chinese stars. When the artist enacted *The Heavenly Maiden Scattering Flowers* and I was in the audience delighting in his airy movements as he sang and danced, I was altogether ignorant of the prodigious amount of energy the actor was expending. Afterwards, I learned that perspiration had moistened his clothing.'

Thousands of critiques and laudatory articles like the foregoing may be found in Chinese newspapers and magazines, and while it is tempting to reproduce them all, yet the nature of our book permits the inclusion of only one more. The detailed catalogue of the merits of Mr. Mei, as written by the aged scholar Mr. Hsiu Mo, treats his subject with a thoroughness that may not be found, perhaps, in similar writings in other parts of the world. A translation follows:

"In the springtime, I went with friends to the Chi Hsiang Theatre. About a week afterwards, I completed a critique on Mr. Mei's marvellous acting and his art. While a complete record of the many merits of Mr. Mei would be a superhuman task, I offer here sixteen points as they come into my mind:

The Face

"Mr. Mei's facial expression and his intelligent use of the same may be compared with the adaptability of running water, which, placed in a square receptacle, is square, but when put in a round one, is round.

The Stage Walk

"The exquisite beauty of the actor's stage walk has been praised elsewhere. In the drama *The Betrothal at the Bright Tower*, Mr. Mei sings as he walks, never increasing or decreasing the length of his footsteps by a fraction of an inch; while in other plays, such as *Picking the Mulberry* and *Washing the Yarn*, his manner of walking is the spirit of animation.

The Waist

"Mr. Tse-ching once said: 'Every one knows of the beauty of Mr. Mei's stage walk, but who knows that much of its grace lies in the use of the waist? Sheer beauty lies in the waist, which stands strong and erect like a pavilion on a mountain side. He is like a sail fluttering in the brisk breeze, his feet pacing in dainty animation.' All this would be impossible without a perfectly controlled waist. This particular accomplishment was heaven-given, a boon not to be acquired, which the artist has cultivated and improved by assiduous practice.

Declamation

"There are innumerable kinds of declamation. Not only has Mr. Mei mastered all styles, but the clarity of his enunciation is the joy of critics.

Acting

"I have heard it said that the artist's acting is beautiful beyond words. How can weak words do justice to his superb art? The words 'unhurried' and 'willing' (to give his best) may, after a fashion, be applied to his acting.

The Smile

"There is the coy smile, the sudden smile, a forced laugh, and an unpremeditated laugh, as in *Rainbow Pass*. Some of the new plays show the actor smiling in a charmingly innocent mood.

Weeping

"When the actor weeps with lowered head, the audience are moved to grief, and all fail in their attempt to applaud because of the tears that fall and wet their sleeves.

Emotional Expression

"To express joy is easy, but to mirror deep tragedy is extremely difficult. The anger shown in the first part of *The Wild Goose Barrier*, the fear manifested in the eyes in the second part, and that evinced in the third part when entering the palace hall make the body quiver. Also there is the joy of a wife meeting her husband after eighteen years of separation.

The Stage Death

"'In the labyrinth of stage convention,' says Prince Hung Tou, 'the act of dying is the most difficult. Too much or too little realism mar the desired impression. Mr. Mei, however, gives a perfect conventional representation. His four limbs relax or stiffen as he seems to lose all consciousness.'

The Use of the Sleeve

"Fluttering like a frightened swan, swift like a sportive butterfly, the turning or the folding of the sleeve about the wrist of Mr. Mei has been reduced to a fine art. He may drop it speedily like a sail or make it dart like an arrow lightly and animatedly from its bow. Other actors complain of the excessive length of the attached inner sleeves, while Mr. Mei sometimes thinks his too short.

The Dance

"In *Kuei-fei Intoxicated with Wine* there is the biting of the rim of the beaker and the bending of the waist while the giddy beauty drinks strong wine. In *Ch'ang O's Flight to the Moon*, there is the raising of the skirt and the flourishing of the sleeves, all of which the actor does in accordance with the strict conventional requirements of rhythm.

Vocal Art

"The *érh-huang* style is alluring, while the *hsi-p'i* is grave and majestic. From these two old models, Mr. Mei has remoulded and created new musical scores. The *hsi-p'i* must be handled with utmost care, for the method of vocalization demands both a decided style of melody and a mastery of enunciation. . . .

Music with the Flute

"The intricate k'un-ch'ü musical style demands absolute adherence to time, the greater part of the singing being done in a low, well-modulated voice. Mr. Mei has not only spent much time in the study of this art but has had the assistance of the best masters of the style in the country. . . . An old and very conservative critic of the theatre once said to me: 'Have you heard Mei's k'un-ch'ü monodrama, *A Nun Seeks Love*? There is genuine merit in the singing and the acting.'

Postures in Sword-Horse Rôles

"Since the presentation some time ago of the military plays, *The River Fan Pass*, *Rainbow Pass*, etc., Mr. Mei's gymnastical postures have acquired a remarkable finish, and his handling of weapons has become both masterful and heroic. While executing the foregoing action, he also sings with much subtlety of expression concerning love or any emotion the text of the drama may call for.

The *Wu*, or Military Plays

"After the production of *The Red-Robed Empress*, Mr. Mei impersonated the heroines of *Golden Mountain Monastery* and *The Fairy of the Guitar*—rôles offering a direct contrast to the gentle operatic heroines which the actor portrayed early in his career. A hard-working youth, this theatrical idol has enlarged his field of interpretation until he is now the leading exponent of feminine stage types. . . .

Modernized Old Dramas

"In the dance drama *Ch'ang O's Flight to the Moon*, the actor offers his public novelties in make-up and costume. The play is done in good taste.

Youthful Portraits of the Actor in Chinese Dress

Mr. Mei Lan-fang in European Attire

It would require thousands of words to give an adequate description of his supreme art. In both singing and declamation, Mr. Mei is never guilty of a slurred syllable, or of poor acting. In short, a moment with Mei is better than years with other actors!"

Our account would be incomplete without mention of the triumphal visits the actor occasionally makes to the leading cities of China.

An early story, undoubtedly from a Chinese newspaper cutting, narrates a typical incident in the celebrity's life, on his visit to that most famous spot of scenic beauty, the renowned West Lake, with its city of Hangchow. The following account was written:

"Once Mr. Mei Lan-fang acted in a playhouse in the city of Hangchow, where the stage door opened on an empty lot that could accommodate thousands of people. On the day in question, when the actor had completed his performance and was about to leave, the entire space was filled with expectant and admiring people crowded 'shoulder to shoulder, and toes to toes.' Every one was eager and thirsting for a glimpse of the artist! The public has never accorded such an ovation to other actors."

But there is nothing in the annals of the Chinese stage to compare with the actor's engagements in Shanghai, of which two only, those of 1926 and 1928, will be mentioned. As is true in the life of public idols the world over, excessive admiration is never an unmixed blessing.

The opening night of the 1926 engagement, Monday, November 15, was described in the *North-China Daily News* as follows:

"On Monday evening last, Mr. Mei Lan-fang opened his engagement at the Ta-hsin Wu-t'ai. As early as 7 p.m., great crowds thronged the streets near the theatre. The audience is said to have numbered over three thousand. Banks of flowers, sent by admirers, filled the entrance; while above hung a gigantic floral plaque with the three characters 梅蘭芳 [Mei Lan-fang] worked in pink satin."

On his departure, the actor was inundated with gifts in the form of flowers, paintings, silver cups, silver services, silver plaques inscribed with the names of the donors, specimens of calligraphy, couplets written on eight-foot lengths of silk, and so on — all of which, according to established theatrical custom, were exhibited at the sides of the stage on the farewell night.

If the foregoing paragraphs give the impression that Mr. Mei's life is an Elysian dream or the proverbial bed of roses, it is only necessary to cite a few of the incidents which marred what might have been an unmixed joy. To be dined and wined all hours of the day and much of the night; to feel unable to refuse many invitations; to grace a banquet table and be gazed at when one's physician has ordered rest in bed, not to take into account that performances last well after midnight, after which the actor is besieged by admirers — all help to prove that most celebrities pay and overpay for their fame. Those who may still enjoy the inestimable boons of privacy and the choice to do as they wish envy the fame of those who would, perhaps, give up everything for the peace in which one is his own master and not the object at which are directed a thousand attentions, well-meant or otherwise.

The 1928 Shanghai engagement, which opened on December 17, repeated the triumphs along with the mixed blessings of 1926. From the two leading Chinese daily newspapers, which kept the eager public informed as to everything the actor did in a special column, one quotation will give an idea of Mr. Mei's routine. For Wednesday, December 19, the *Mei News* in the *Shun Pao* read as follows: " The Nanyang Brothers' Tobacco Company, on Mr. Mei's going to Canton, presented him with a magnificent curtain of imperial yellow satin, decorated with the branch of an ancient plum tree. . . . The company also presented the actor with a silver cup. . . .

" Several callers [named] visited the actor in his hotel.

A Shady, Red-Lacquered Colonnade Leading to the Mei House

"Friends sent Mei a huge silver cup. . . . The actor first attended Mr. Mu's party, thereafter keeping another appointment in Nanyang Road before going to the theatre. . . .

"A request was made of the actor that he write a title to be used on the cover of a publication, which he granted. A representative of a pictorial magazine arrived at the hotel to photograph Mr. Mei. . . .

"Mr. Nieh gave a dinner for Messrs. Mei Lan-fang and Wang Feng-ching."

Thus in China, which to outsiders is already colourful, the public life of Mr. Mei Lan-fang is a constant kaleidoscope of colours. That part of the occident which has never crossed the Pacific or gone beyond Suez will marvel at the unique grace and distinctive flavour that is the art of Mr. Mei. It will see an art that "out-adjectives" all the indefinite effusions used in the past to paint an imaginary sketch of the Flowery Kingdom.

When you visit noble Peking, do not fail to see the actor among his own people. China will welcome you, as will also Mr. Mei Lan-fang.

The Bodhisattva P'u-hsien, painted by Mr. Mei Lan-fang

APPENDIX

APPENDIX

A Brief Consideration of the Outstanding Characteristics of the Chinese Drama

By
Professor Chi Jushan

Parts 1 and 2
By
Mr. Huang Chiu-yao

Translated by
George Kin Leung

CONTENTS

PART 1

The Character Types of the Chinese Drama

Male Types: *Lao-shêng*; *Hsiao-shêng*; *Wên-shêng*; *Wu-shêng* — Female Types: *Lao-tan* *Ch'ing-i*; *Hua-tan*; *Kuei-mên-tan*; *Tao-ma-tan* — Painted-Face Types: *Wu-ching*; Prince Lan-ling — Comedian Types: *Ch'ou-tan*; *Wu-ch'ou*; T'ang Ming Huang as a Comedian . . 81-83

PART 2

A Musical Division of Chinese Drama

K'un-Ch'ü: Historical Sketch; Types of Current Chinese Music; High Quality of Style; Mr. Mei's Service to *K'un-ch'ü*; Comparison of *K'un-ch'ü* and *P'i-huang* — The Anhwei Musical Style, or *Hui Tiao*; Historical Sketch; Local Schools of Drama; Comparison of Anhwei and Peking Drama — *P'i-huang*: Historical Sketch 84-87

PART 3

Characteristics of the Chinese Drama

Singing and Declamation — The Prologue, or *Yin-tzŭ* — Couplets When Entering, or *Shang Ch'ang Tui Chü* — Poetry While Sitting, or *Tso Shih* — Announcing One's Name, *T'ung Ming* — Lines that Open the Play, or *Ting Ch'ang Pai* — The Aside, or *Pei Kung* — The "Call," or Signal for Music, or *Chiao Pan* — Singing, or *Ko Ch'ang* — Couplets Recited Before Going Off the Stage, or *Hsia Ch'ang Tui Lien* 88-92

PART 4

Pantomime and Acting

Entrance and Exit — Walking and Running — Passing Through a Door — Movement in General — Tea Drinking — Taking Wine and Rice — Sleeping — The Art of Dancing — Conventional Stage Fighting — Miscellaneous Actions 93-96

PART 5

Costumes of the Chinese Stage

The Robe, or *Mang* — The Official Robe, or *Kuan I* — The *P'ei* — The Lined Coat, or *Tieh-tzŭ* — The Eunuch's Coat, or *T'ai Chien I* — The Jade Belt, or *Yü Tai* — The Skirt, or *Ch'ün* — The Jacket and Trousers, or

APPENDIX

K'u Ao — The Vest, or K'an Chien — Costumes for Palace Women, or Kung I — The Tasselled Cape, or Yün Chien — The Storm Cloak, or Tou Fêng — A Modern Tieh-tzǔ, or Shih Shih Tieh-tzǔ — The Manchu Coat, or Ch'i I — Warrior's Regalia, or K'ai K'ao — The Ordinary Official Robe, or K'ai Ch'ang — Military Flags, or K'ao Ch'i — The Fighting Costume, or Ta I — The Arrow Costume, or Chien I — The Short Jacket, or Ma Kua — The Glass Abdomen, or Pien K'ao — The Eight-Figured Diagram Robe, or Pa Kua I — The Dragon Robe, or Lung T'ao I — The Ancient Costume, or Ku Chuang — Animal Costumes, or Shou I — Weeds of Mourning, or Shang Fu I 97-104

PART 6

Headgear and Footwear

The Helmet or Hat, or K'uei — The Gauze Hat, or Sha Mao — The Soft Hat, or Chin — The Military Hat, or Lo Mao — The Phœnix Hat, or Fêng Kuan — The Wind Hat, or Fêng Mao — Pheasant Plumes, or Chih Wei — Fox-Tails, or Hu Wei — Shoes and Boots, or Hsüeh Hsieh . . 105-107

PART 7

Beards and Moustaches, or Hu Hsü

The Full Beard, or Man Jan — The Tripart Beard, or San Jan — The Short Moustache, or Tuan Jan — Miscellaneous Remarks 108-109

PART 8

Stage Properties and Symbolism

The Horse-Whip, or Ma Pien — Wagon Flags, or Ch'ê Ch'i — The Sedan, or Chiao-tzǔ — The Duster, or Ying Ch'ên — The Cloth City Wall, or Pu Chêng — Wind Flags, or Fêng Ch'i — Water Flags, or Shui Ch'i — The Great Curtain, or Ta Chang-tzǔ — Mountain Rocks, or Shan Shih P'ien — The Table, or Cho-tzǔ — The Chair, or I-tzǔ — The Mandate Arrow, or Ling Chien — The Standard, or Fu Chieh — The Long-Handled Fan, or Chang Shan — The Umbrella, or San — The Lantern, or Têng — The Ivory Tablet, or Hu — Miscellaneous Objects — Stage Clouds, or Yün P'ien — The Flag on Top of a Soldier's Spear, or Mên Ch'iang Ch'i — Military Weapons, or Ping Ch'i 110-116

PART 9

Musical Instruments

The Wooden Time Beater, or Pan — The Small Drum, or Hsiao Ku — The Great Drum, or Ta Ku — The Chinese Violin, or Hu-ch'in — The Moon Guitar, or Yüeh-ch'in — The Three-Stringed Guitar, or Hsien-tzǔ — The Flute, or Ti-tzǔ — The Reed Organ, or Shêng — The Two-Stringed Hu, or Êrh-hu — The Four-Stringed Hu, or Ssǔ-hu — The Clarinet, or So Na — The Gong, or Lo — Cymbals, or Nao — The Small Gong, or Hsiao Lo — The Bell, or P'êng Chung — The Nine-Toned Gong, or Chiu Yin Lo 117-121

APPENDIX

Part I

THE CHARACTER TYPES OF THE CHINESE DRAMA

The Male Characters, or *Shêng*
(生)

The male rôles in old Chinese drama are collectively known as *shêng*. Aged and bearded characters are designated as "old," or *lao-shêng* (老生), while youthful male characters are known as "youthful," or *hsiao-shêng* (小生). All who specialize in diction and singing are termed "civil," or *wên-shêng* (文生); those skilled in gymnastics and military action are known as "military," or *wu-shêng* (武生). In the singing of a *wên-shêng*, a most important consideration is that all high and low notes should be sung in the best style, while a thorough mastery of vocal technique is necessary, because, in the drama, the types of singing are exceedingly numerous. A *lao-shêng*, often the rôle of a scholar or a general, must be proficient in conventional stage technique. In his enunciation, he must be fastidiously correct, while, in acting, he must possess grace, dignity, and distinction; above all, he must not overdo his part. The *wu-shêng* specializes in bodily posture and in conventional stage fighting; the movement of his hands and feet must be clean-cut and his manner of expression good. He is also expected to be an expert tumbler and acrobat. A *wên-shêng* (文生) should be refined and cultured in a worldly fashion.

The Female Impersonator, or *Tan*
(旦)

The general term in old drama for all feminine rôles is *tan*, meaning female impersonator. There are the "old," or *lao-tan* (老旦), who may be mothers or other aged women; *ch'ing-i* (青衣), the rôles for good and dignified women; *hua-tan* (花旦), the rôles for vivacious maidservants or women of doubtful reputation, as the demi-mondaine and courtesan; *kuei-mên-tan* (閨門旦), the type for maidens; and the *tao-ma* (刀馬), or "sword-horse," *tan*, who is a "military" type.

APPENDIX

Of these types there is a fuller account in Chapter III, where some paragraphs have been quoted from the article, "The Female Impersonator of the Chinese Stage," reprinted by courtesy of the *China Journal*.

The Characters with Painted Faces, or C*hing*
(淨)

Actors portraying the character type known in the stage vernacular as *ching*, must be coarse and heavy in physique and possess voices that are rich and robust, while their movements must be dignified. In the bewildering variety of facial painting, there are both fine-lined and thick-lined designs. If one is a *wu-ching* (武淨), he must also be a master of boxing, gymnastics, and conventional military action.

While gentle and peace-loving characters appear with natural faces, others, especially adventurers, commonly paint their faces in various styles that range from a single colour to bewildering combinations and figures. The origin of facial painting may be traced to ancient stone sculptures and bronze engravings; but, as time passed, the original art underwent radical changes. Many of the colours have a specific meaning; for instance, a predominance of red indicates that the person is courageous, faithful, and virtuous; much black indicates a brusque nature; while blue denotes cruelty. Green, blue, lavender, and red, when used in elaborate combination, have no deep significance. A person with triangular eyes is branded as crafty, while a person with a small white butterfly painted across his nose may be a comedian, a villain, or an evil supernatural being. Again, the face may be painted in ways that have no special meaning.

During the Northern Chi dynasty (550-565), Prince Lan-ling, or Lan-ling Wang, who was a brave warrior with an exquisitely beautiful face, conceived the idea of painting his face to inspire fear in the hearts of his adversaries. It is possible that conventional facial painting for the stage originated from this source.

The Comedian, or Ch'*ou*
(丑)

The general term for comedians is *ch'ou*, a type which is common on both the Chinese and the European stage. Those who are supposed to be *comédiennes* are called *ch'ou-tan* (丑旦), or "female *ch'ou*"; while comedians of military type are called *wu-ch'ou* (武丑). To show that they are comedians, this class, with minor exceptions, paint their noses powder-white, along with a few black lines. Although, at times, other lines may be added to the face, the most common design is the butterfly.

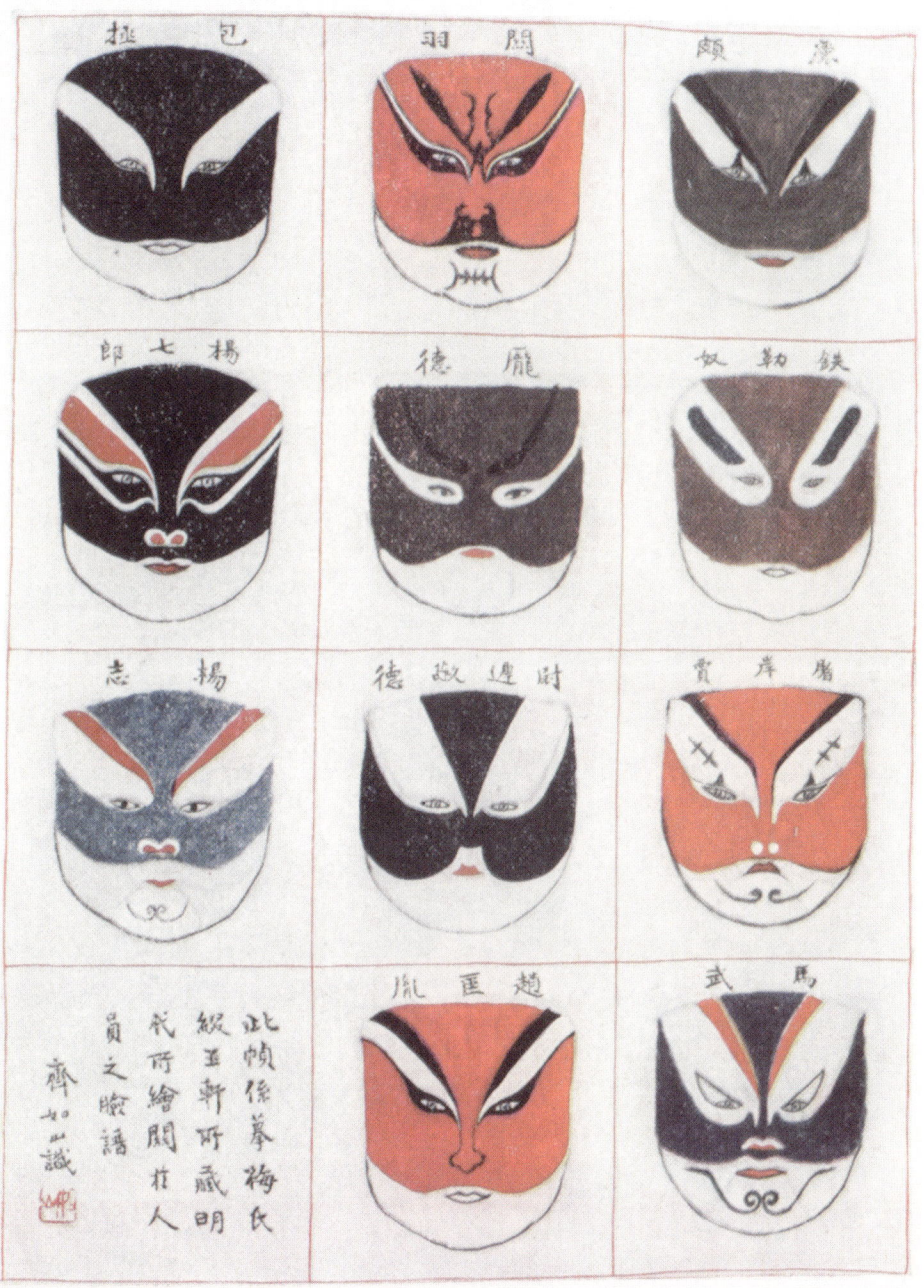

Facial Paintings, Ming Period (1368-1644), Representing Well-Known Characters in History and Fiction

Stage Representations of Lesser Deities and Supernatural Beings, Ming Period (1368-1644)

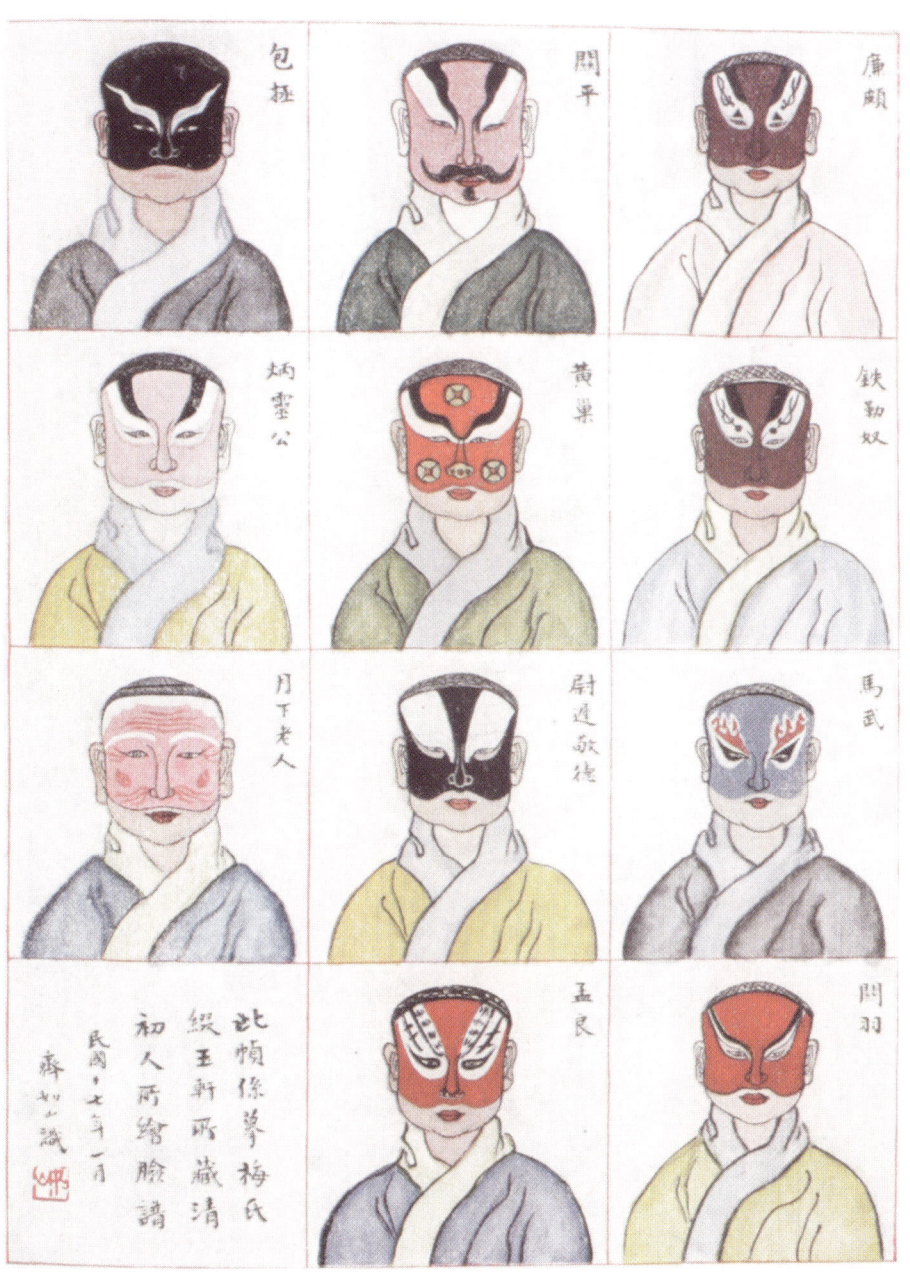

Stage Heroes as Painted in the Ch'ing Dynasty (1644-1911)
This and the preceding two plates are reproductions of paintings from the Mei Library.

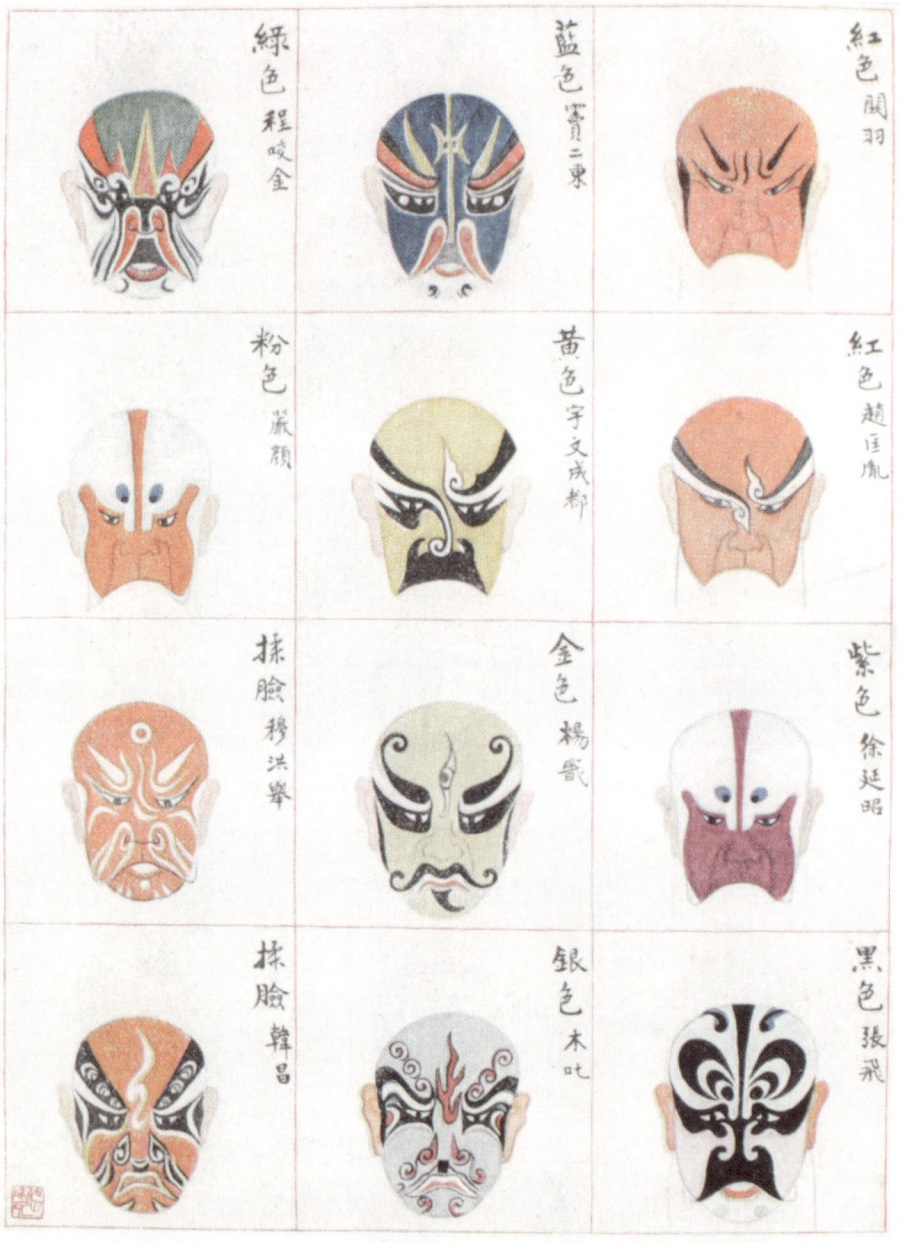

Examples of Facial Painting Now in Vogue on the Peking Stage

Styles of Present-Day Facial Painting

破臉 姜維	破臉 夏侯淵	小白粉臉 蔣幹
破臉 賀化	大白粉臉 曹操	小尖粉臉 朱光祖
破臉 鄧子朗	半白粉臉 嚴世蕃	帶赭色臉 李克用
破臉 常刋	三白粉臉 伯嚭	

以上三幀為現行臉譜之大凡析為兩類一為試色一舉句法至勾法亦每種各佔句法一二舉餘可類推但各伶之繪事亦有出入亦無須臚列其詳當於繪譜時分長風竹竹青以諸其參酌勁頭有規規較法不有

民國廿七年春陸公識

Styles of Present-Day Facial Painting

THE CHARACTER TYPES OF THE CHINESE DRAMA

The comedian's main burden is to win laughs from the audience; thus, his lines must be especially well enunciated, sparkling with wit, and otherwise attractive. If he displays military action, it must be humorous in nature. When a play has in it a first-class comedian, the entire work vibrates with life. The *ch'ou*, then, occupies an important place in the drama. Furthermore, legend informs us that the great ruler, T'ang Ming Huang himself, sometimes played the part of the *ch'ou*, which type as a result has acquired great prestige and is allowed many privileges denied other actors.

PART 2

A MUSICAL DIVISION OF CHINESE DRAMA

The K'un-ch'ü

(崑曲)

The beginnings of crude drama arose from the combination of various arts, dating as far back as the Han (206 B.C. to A.D. 221) and Wei (A.D. 221-265) dynasties. It was during the T'ang dynasty (A.D. 618-906) that there were indications of a division into operatic drama and comedy. The Sungs (A.D. 960-1127) prized the comedy above all other forms of drama. The drama itself, however, became a vehicle for depicting old stories, the most important factors being neither acting nor singing. This type of play was predominant during the Yüan dynasty (A.D. 1280-1368), when the barbarian Hu tribes from the north entered and gained mastery of China, bringing their own drama, which became very popular in the North. In the southern provinces, however, such as Kiangsu and Chekiang, the *literati* studied and adapted this music, creating what is called the Southern School of Music. Hence, what is called *k'un-ch'ü* resulted from the combination of northern and southern music.

The current drama in China is of many types, namely, the *p'i-huang*, the *k'un-ch'ü*, and the *chen-ch'iang*, etc. The upper classes favour the *k'un-ch'ü* drama, because there are strict rules for its acting and singing. As for the *p'i-huang* style, an intelligent actor may, within its general rules, make innovations, as, for instance, the lengthening of certain notes and the addition of extemporized passages. Thus it has come about that various schools of singing have been established by well-known vocalists, who make their main appeal to the ear of the general public.

We find that most of the texts and music of *k'un-ch'ü* dramas have been written by the foremost scholars and musicians of the day. The lyrics and songs are strikingly beautiful. When stories are dramatized, they are more exquisite when done in the *k'un-ch'ü* than when done in the *p'i-huang* style. Few, however, can appreciate the intricacies of the more refined *k'un-ch'ü*, and so, within the last few centuries, this musical style has fallen into disfavour. Since the *p'i-huang* was sung in the Peking dialect, which was used by the members of the court during the reign of the Manchus, and since northerners did not understand the southern *k'un-ch'ü*, it naturally followed that the *p'i-huang* gained a firm-rooted popularity.

A MUSICAL DIVISION OF CHINESE DRAMA

Mr. Mei, appreciating the merits of the *k'un-ch'ü*, devoted special effort to the study of that style. He quickly reinstated the more typical Chinese drama with the better classes of society. The best plays of this type, presented by Mei, are *The Jade Hairpin* and *Sporting by Dream in a Garden*. Coming from the pens of the *literati*, such dramas are, in point of written text and dramatic expression, flawless. The acting and the singing, done according to inviolable rule, are both refined and subtle in expression, especially when done by an actor of Mr. Mei's intelligence. Largely through his inspiration, an association for the special study of the *k'un-ch'ü* has been established in Peking, while in Shanghai there is also a school devoted to the same purpose. Many of the upper classes spend their leisure studying this musical style.

The *p'i-huang* has, as its main instrument, the *hu-ch'in*, which came to China from the North; while the *k'un-ch'ü*, to put the phrase in the words of the Chinese writer, is "drama that Han [China] itself had." This quieter and truly Chinese music is dominated by the soft notes of the flute. The more strident *hu-ch'in* has no place in *k'un-ch'ü* plays, while the soft slow measures of the Chinese music are in direct contrast to the high-pitched and sustained *p'i-huang* melodies. Since there is no ear-splitting brass in the *k'un-ch'ü*, foreigners who come to China enjoy these plays. Yet, the *k'un-ch'ü*, with its superior music and admirable enunciation, is no match for the *p'i-huang*, which is so firmly established with the masses as to defy all competition!

The Anhwei Musical Style, or *Hui Tiao*
(徽調)

The *êrh-huang* and the *hsi-p'i* came originally from Hupeh; these styles, however, underwent modification at the hands of certain scholars in the following cities of Anhwei, namely, Shihmen, Tungcheng, Hsiuning, etc., and so the style came to be known as the Anhwei style. During the reign of K'ang Hsi (1662-1722), large numbers of officials in the capital were natives of Anhwei, bringing with them their own music, which many of the Pekingese learned. The Peking drama of to-day is a direct combination of the music of Hupeh and Anhwei.

Here we may consider an all-important factor in China, namely, the vast extent of the empire which has encouraged the development of many distinct dialects so that each district has also developed its own drama, sung in its own dialect, those of Hupeh and Anhwei being but two types of many, but they are the most popular. Apart from them, there are the *i-yang* drama of Szechwan; the *kao* of Kaoyang, Chihli; the *ch'en* of Chenchung, Shensi; the *yüeh-tiao* of Kwangtung; while Chekiang, Ningpo, Shaoshing, etc., each has its own school of drama and music. This paper, however, is devoted to a consideration of the Anhwei school only, because it is the parent of the present Peking drama, or what Europeans call Chinese drama. It is not the province of this work to describe the many local schools of drama.

Pure Anhwei drama may be found in that province to-day, and it is entirely different from the Peking *p'i-huang* drama. In the first year of K'ang Hsi, the actor, Cheng Chang-keng, a native of Anhwei, enjoyed public favour. There was only the slightest suggestion of Anhwei accent in his singing and declamation. The gap between the singing of female impersonators of the Peking and Anhwei schools is more marked. The simple and clear-cut songs in the *lao-shêng* dramas were not so melodious as those of the present.

The costumes worn in Anhwei and Peking drama are similar; but the former are plain and lack charm because of inadequate preparation. The music played at the opening of an Anhwei drama, while quite unlike that of the Peking drama, is nevertheless very pleasant to the ear. After the preliminary music, one act of *k'un-ch'ü*, in which every member of the company must appear, is offered. This is termed the "first appearance." The regular drama comes afterwards.

In an Anhwei company, there are only twenty to thirty people. When in certain plays there is a shortage of actors, even the super-numeraries, whose humble duty it is to carry the flags, are obliged to take important rôles. This is done by turn and not by the direction of the stage-manager. Of the well-known and popular plays of this school, a striking example is Mr. Mei's beloved *Three Pulls*.

The All-Popular *P'i-huang*
(皮 黃)

The *p'i-huang*, which is a combination of the *hsi-p'i* and *êrh-huang* styles, is now the most popular musical drama of the current stage. The *êrh-huang* comes from Hupeh and receives its name from the fact that many actors come from the districts of Huangkang and Huangpi. The former president, Li Yuan-hung, was a native of Huangpi, and the greatest of all *lao-shêng*, Tan Shen-pei, was also a native of Huangpi. He was acknowledged the "Great King of Actors." Since his death, the kingship has passed on to Mr. Mei Lan-fang. The *êrh-huang*, now naturalized in the Peking drama, is popular throughout China.

In the spoken lines of such dramas, a correctly declaimed passage should contain Hupeh accents. The *p'i-huang* was an immediate success with the general public and still is. In this school of drama, there are a few thousand plays, each a vehicle for the display of the talents of various stage types, as the *shêng, tan, ching, ch'ou*, etc. The *p'i-huang* is always the musical basis for plays, even those written for well-known actors of to-day. It is easy to keep time with the music of the *p'i-huang*. Now that the *k'un-ch'ü* has experienced a revival, this style and the *p'i-huang* have their respective followings.

The lyrics of *p'i-huang* music are set mainly to the *hu-ch'in*, the technique of which has been developed largely by master musicians. Tunes have both changed and increased in variety. Mr. Mei's paternal uncle, Yu-tien, was the greatest *hu-ch'in* player of the last two decades.

The *p'i-huang* came into vogue in the Hsien-Fêng (1851-1861) period, when the Anhwei actor, Cheng Chang-keng, presented his *êrh-huang* Anhwei dramas in the capital, where his innovation met with warm welcome. Thereafter, four large training schools for actors were established. Mr. Mei's grandfather, Mr. Mei Chiao-ling, also a female impersonator of note, was head of the Ssŭ-hsi Training School, which was the largest of the four institutions. Graduates of these schools have gone forth spreading the Peking drama over China and bringing the fame of the Chinese stage to a grand climax. Most of the discussions of music and conventions in this chapter are concerned with the Peking School of Drama.

PART 3
CHARACTERISTICS OF THE CHINESE DRAMA

Singing and Declamation

The spoken lines and vocal passages of the Chinese drama are, generally speaking, similar to those of other nations. When a Chinese actor, however, comes upon the stage, he must deliver what is termed the prologue, and perhaps poetry also, as well as lines of a couplet. The *tien-chiang-ch'un* tunes (點絳脣), used by those who impersonate officials, are similar in construction to the prologue just mentioned. An actor, on gracefully making his way off the stage, may recite any one or more of the following: poetry, lines of a couplet, or passages of recitative. These distinctive practices on entering and exit are characteristics which set the Chinese drama apart from that of any other nation. The stage speech is invariably marked by cadence and rhythm and so differs, in a marked degree, from that of everyday life. Although, in the drama of every nation there is a decided difference between the speech of the stage and real life, the difference, in Chinese drama, is much greater. In vocal art each country has its own musical scale; and there are inevitable differences in the scales of various nations. In Chinese drama, the actor's movements also are set to musical accompaniment; in European plays there exists no such practice. So far, an attempt has been made to point out the difference, in general, between Chinese and European drama. Details of this will be found under the headings that follow.

The Prologue, or *Yin-tzŭ*
(引子)

When an actor makes his entrance, the first words he utters are what is technically known as the prologue, which literally "introduces" or brings forward the idea of the play. There is, during the recitation, a distinct rhythm; but there is no musical accompaniment, even the wooden *pan-tzŭ* not being used to beat time. The prologue found its origin in the extreme dislike of mentioning at once and directly the subject of a literary work. Thus, in drama, introductory lines are added to uphold this tradition, the prologue doing one of the following things: it may narrate vaguely the entire action of the play, tell the history or nature of the character in question, or explain the general action of the act immediately at hand. But whatever is the case, there is delivered merely a general account, from which one may trace little or no clue to the actual story.

CHARACTERISTICS OF THE CHINESE DRAMA 89

Couplets When Entering, or *Shang Ch'ang Tui Chü*
(上場對句)

After the prologue, actors invariably recite two couplets, this seeming to be a development of the prologue. At the beginning, the *ch'ou*, or comedian, used couplets more than any other character type, for the simple reason that it was permissible for comedians to speak in the various local dialects of the districts in which they were acting. Thus, he was not obliged to use the Chung-chou intonations on the endings of his monosyllables. The Chung-chou, being the standard combination of intonations, are used in Honan and in the central part of China. Since a comedian found it inconvenient to recite these intonations, he substituted couplets in the native dialect, at the same time doing away with tempo and musical accompaniment. In order to facilitate action, it came about afterward that all types of actors on entering the stage recited the more easily delivered couplets.

Poetry While Sitting, or *Tso Shih*
(坐詩)

After the prologue, and sometimes couplets also, have been delivered, the actor, seating himself, recites four lines of poetry, which are technically termed "poetry that opens the play." In idea and construction, this same practice, also called "poetry while sitting," bears a close resemblance to the prologue. Its origin comes from the style of the Chinese novel, or an entertainment known as "recitations with the drum," *ku-tz'ŭ* (鼓詞), in which forms there are always at the opening of the work a few lines which outline the entire theme. The dramas of the Yüan and Sung dynasties were strikingly similar in construction to the novel and "recitations with the drum," and thus plays have introductory lines also. While the *kun-ch'ü* employs lines of uneven length, the *p'i-huang* uses a poetical text exclusively. "Poetry while sitting" differs from the prologue in that the actor must recite without tempo, and without musical accompaniment.

Announcing One's Name, or *Tung Ming*
(通名)

After an actor has recited his four lines of poetry, he never fails to tell the audience his name, and if he does not recite poetry, he may announce his name immediately after the delivery of the prologue.

Lines that Actually Open the Play, or *Ting Ch'ang Pai*
(定場白)

The technical term *pai* (白) means to express, to explain, to speak. An actor, having gone on the stage and spoken both his prologue and poetic lines and having announced his name, then proceeds to deliver what is termed the *ting ch'ang pai*. That the prologue, poetry, etc., must be very general in nature has already been explained; in the *ting ch'ang pai*, however, an actor gives a detailed account of himself, or his family, or the drama, often of the immediate act or episode at hand, making such facts clear in minute detail. If the action of the present moment is too far removed from that of the preceding event, it behooves the actor to explain this state of affairs while delivering the *ting ch'ang pai*.

In French drama, there is often a person not belonging to the cast of the play, who, standing in front of the curtain, delivers lines that are similar to the *ting ch'ang pai*. After a Chinese actor has delivered his *ting ch'ang pai*, the actual play begins to unfold. While the actor recites the prologue, poetry, and the *ting ch'ang pai*, he is mirroring the general feeling of the action or the theme of the play. Although, in subsequent acts, there may be another announcement of the name, yet, according to old practice, this came into being merely because some of the episodes were too far apart and also because the changing of costume might lead to the audience's forgetting the names of the various characters. Thus the actor sometimes once more announces his name. The ancients, however, found for such situations remedies slightly different from those employed at present.

The four foregoing practices are, in the construction of the old Chinese drama, distinctive features, in which it differs signally from European drama. In certain plays in France, in 1907 and 1908, preliminary passages were delivered before the lowered curtain to the audience by a person who was *not* a member of the cast, an announcement sometimes being made previous to each act. In Chinese drama, such lines must be delivered by members of the cast. At one time, there was in Chinese drama a special person who made announcements and was known as the *fu mo chia mên* (副末家門); but he made the briefest remarks only, not at all in the detailed manner of the French stage. Furthermore, he who delivered the prologue in the old drama was obliged to wear a special stage costume, in this respect again differing from foreign practice.

In French drama it was formerly the practice to employ a man in formal dress to make the necessary preliminary explanations; later, because of public demand, the man was replaced by a young girl, beautifully attired. More recently, an improvement has been introduced, wherein the girl sings, before the first curtain, the entire story of the play. This last practice seems to approach more closely the peculiar practices of Chinese drama. In times past, when an actor came on the stage to recite the prologue and announce his name, he was obliged by inviolable custom to conceal his face with his sleeve in order not to reveal the "face of the actor in the play"; but after the announcements have been made, the sleeve is waved aside and, lo! we have before us the actual face or character of the play! The actor has stepped into character. Is there not, in this, a striking similarity to the practices in French drama?

CHARACTERISTICS OF THE CHINESE DRAMA

The Aside, or *Pei Kung*[1]
(背供)

The "aside" may be described as words uttered to oneself in the presence of two or three others on the stage to reveal one's emotion or secrets. If one is suddenly overwrought with emotion, he naturally expresses himself by facial expression or pantomime; if the emotion is so complex that neither facial expression nor pantomime can make clear the meaning, then the Chinese actor lifts his sleeve, behind which he speaks or sings, or he may quickly step to one side of the stage, such actions making it clear that the others on the stage have not heard what was said. When a solitary actor sings or tells of his own affairs, the practice is also somewhat similar to the aside.

The aside is a distinct feature of Chinese drama. Considering the early date at which this dramatic peculiarity was discovered, it must be conceded to be a special merit of native drama. The aside eliminates great quantities of explanation, at the same time adding much interest to the situation. In European drama also, a person may say a few words to himself. Since people in everyday life are known to speak to themselves, the aside may have found its origin in that human trait. In European opera, it is a common practice for one person to sing long solos; this practice has in it something of the nature of an aside.

The "Call" or Signal for Music, or *Chiao Pan*
(叫板)

When all preliminary announcements have been made, the actor, just before breaking into song, must prolong the last word he has spoken. This is done by sustaining the last word, almost to a musical pitch, so that the musicians know by this signal that the song is to come at once and so set their musical instruments for accompaniment. Again, when the actor is about to conclude his singing, he also prolongs the last word or two in his song so that the musicians will know that the song is completed and will prepare to lay aside their instruments. Such vocal prolongations are absolutely necessary, because, in the *p'i-huang* music, there being no arbitrary musical score, it is possible for a singer to prolong or abbreviate his song as he deems fit; thus there must be a distinct signal given by the singer as to when the song will begin or end.

Singing, or *Ko Ch'ang*
(歌唱)

It is a common practice in Chinese drama when, during spoken lines, the emotions become raised to a high pitch, for the character to give vent to his feeling in song, as in

---

[1] The writer of the original Chinese includes the soliloquy under the aside. Furthermore, he does not seem to gather that, in European drama of to-day, the aside is considered a distinct weakness in play construction unless it occurs naturally, as in real life.—G. K. L.

moments of sudden fear, anger, grief, or ecstasy. Again, there are occasions when long dramatic passages must be repeated by the actors, this also serving as a reason for a long aria. If one character asks another about a matter of which the latter is ignorant, but of which the audience has been already informed, there is a possibility of the patience of the audience being tried by tedious repetition. The reply, therefore, is set to music so that the actor may have the opportunity to explain the situation, and to embellish his tale with such musical beauty as to save the audience monotonous repetition.

In singing, there is a wide variety of style for the character types. For instance, the *hua-lien* (花臉), or "flowery-faced one," so called in reference to the elaborate facial painting, sings in broad, rich, robust tones to delineate a brusque character; the *shêng* sings in an almost natural voice, which labels him as an educated and refined person; while the *tan* sings in a falsetto voice in order to suggest the voice of a woman. As there is a vast amount of detail of this nature, one may, while witnessing an actual performance, use his own imagination and fathom the meanings for himself. Therefore, we will not go into further details.

Couplets Recited Before Going Off the Stage, or *Hsia Ch'ang Tui Lien*
（下場對聯）

After an actor has played his part and is about to move off the stage, it is customary for him to recite four lines, namely, two couplets; or if two or more people go off together, they may recite four lines of poetry. These recitations are supposed to conclude the act or scene in question. Such peculiar practices trace their origin to the literary form of the old Chinese novel.

PART 4
PANTOMIME AND ACTING

Every movement made by an actor in an old Chinese drama is done in accordance with time-honoured convention, and so it is somewhat different from the actions of everyday life. Although in European and American plays the actions are also different from those of ordinary life, still the difference in Chinese drama is much greater. An attempt will now be made to explain some of the Chinese stage conventions and to point out where they differ from Western theatrical practice.

Entrance and Exit

In European drama, the various actors, before the curtain goes up, have usually placed themselves in appropriate positions on the stage; and they proceed, as soon as the curtain has been raised, with the immediate action or conversation of the play. The Chinese drama opens with an empty stage, on which the various characters make their appearance. Before their entrance, there is an orchestral selection, and most of the movements of the actors are made to definite musical setting. All action, even the simple act of walking, must be done gracefully and to a well-defined tempo, which may or may not be set to musical accompaniment. The tempo is determined by the musicians. When an actor makes his first appearance, it is highly important that his every movement be pleasing to the eye, while every action is dictated by inviolable rule. It is required that an actor, on making his exit with either declamation or singing, leave one word unsaid, until with body slightly turned to the audience, he declaims or sings it just before he turns to walk off the stage. The exit must also be done to musical accompaniment.

Walking and Running

In the drama of every nation, actors, while on the stage, walk differently from people in everyday life; in Chinese drama, the difference is even more striking. Yet the highly conventional gait of the various character types has a logical origin. The brusque types walk with long strides, and so the *hua-lien* takes steps that are technically termed "wide." Both scholars and officials invariably move about with marked grace and leisure; thus, the gait of the *shêng* is described as "round," "square," or "dexterous"; while female characters, or *tan*, walk with short, swaying, mincing steps, described as "slow," "graceful," etc. But it matters not which character type is on the stage, he must take his steps in accordance with strictly determined tempo; in situations demanding quick movement, there is the "swift tempo," while for slow gait, there is the "slow tempo," and never for a moment does an actor of any merit dare to depart from that tempo.

APPENDIX

Passing Through a Door

Whenever it is necessary for an actor to enter through a doorway, he merely indicates that he has done so by lifting one foot as if stepping over the door-sill; while female characters raise the hand to show that they are leaning against the wall for support, this being a means of revealing the delicate grace that is associated with the weaker sex. It matters not whether one enters or exits by the front door, the room door, or the garden door, the pantomimic action is the same. The actor merely indicates that he has opened or closed a door; with both hands, he pushes the imaginary panels of the door, sliding them apart or drawing them together. In cases of knocking, bolting, or locking a door, these actions are indicated by pantomimic gesture also.

Movement in General

Chinese actors must give undivided attention to every movement. Action must not only be good to look upon but also done according to strict tempo. The manner in which the head is moved, the body is controlled, the hands and feet are placed, the posture of the arms and thighs—all such action must be done according to established convention. The movement of a finger, the glance of an eye, the lifting of a foot, all entail a vast amount of study, but always these movements must be pleasant to the eye and done to strict tempo.

To make clear this point, one of many examples may be taken, namely, one of the positions of the *tan's* fingers. The index finger is bent back with great strength; the thumb and middle finger form a circle; the ring finger, in Chinese the "no name" finger (無名指), is bent so that the tip rests against the middle joint of the middle finger; while the little finger must be so curved that its tip rests against the middle of the ring finger. This, then, is but one example from the endless number of conventional practices in the old drama. It is highly desirable for one interested in the theatre to attend plays and observe for himself the various peculiarities and develop an ability to make his own fascinating discoveries.

Tea Drinking

The act of tea drinking takes place frequently in Chinese drama. The tea-cup is never put down. The person who pours the tea places the cup in the hand of the recipient. An actor, while drinking, holds his sleeve before his face, because the *shêng*, the male characters, often with beards, would make drinking unpleasant to the eye. Since men drink in this manner, female characters do likewise. Having drunk the tea, the cup is handed back to the servant. There are occasions when a *hua-tan* does not use her sleeve or hand to conceal the act of drinking. This, however, is an act of playfulness, and not at all according to orthodox conventions.

PANTOMIME AND ACTING

Taking Wine and Rice

In the old drama, actors are never shown eating rice or taking a meal, because the sight of eating is considered unpleasing to the eye. A song or a few notes of the flute suffice to indicate that a meal has been taken. If eating must be done, then the drinking of wine may represent the act. Wine is taken in the same manner as tea; but while only one cup of tea may be taken, as many as three cups of wine may be taken consecutively.

Sleeping

In the past, it was not permissible to give a realistic representation of sleep, because the act itself was considered unbeautiful to look upon! When slumber was to be shown, the actor did so by leaning on a table. Maidens, however, may at times be seen sleeping full length, merely because a beauty in slumber is considered a pleasing sight; and so such scenes are created for the especial enjoyment of the spectator. Even this departure from tradition has been made only in recent times. When a *ch'ou*, or comedian, sometimes sleeps, sprawled on a chair, his head thrown back, and his mouth agape, it is understood that this is done merely to win laughs from the audience.

The Art of Dancing

In European drama, it is common to see dancing, unaccompanied by singing, or vice versa; in Chinese drama, however, dancing is accompanied by singing, as well as acting. Again, European musical drama has an especial regard for tempo; Chinese drama requires not only strict adherence to tempo, but also that movements of the dance must harmonize with the idea of the written text; that is, the rhythm and the action must express the musical score as well. It was after Mr. Mei Lan-fang had created his own plays that his school of dancing became popular throughout the entire Chinese Republic. His method of dancing is patterned after the ancient canons of terpsichorean art, said to be over one thousand years old; he has set the movements to the music of to-day, making a real contribution to the stage. This, then, is one of Mr. Mei's greatest services to the drama.

Conventional Stage Fighting

Almost everything on the Chinese stage is symbolical or unrealistic in nature. Conventional stage fighting was introduced during the last century, and consequently is somewhat more realistic. It is worthy of close study. The art of stage fighting lies in *not* touching one's opponent. At first sight, there seems to be no order, merely a confusion of twirlings, brandishings of weapons, and rushings to and fro; but diligent observation shows that every movement is done to strict rule, often taking the form of remarkable synchronizations, which enable an actor's weapon to miss his opponent's head by a hair's-breadth. When hands or weapons are crossed, the battle has actually begun; when actors pass each other close at hand, the action represents the opposing horses of antagonists dashing back and forth; when actors come to a sudden stand, the fighters are taking a rest and awaiting an advantageous moment to move again. It is needless to enumerate all the intricate details; suffice it to say that every little movement, such as crossing the hands, posturing, etc., must be done in accordance with strict tempo.

Miscellaneous Actions

It may be reiterated, in conclusion, that every movement on the Chinese stage is done in accordance with strict, time-honoured convention. For example, when a male character laughs, he does so directly; but a female character must conceal her mouth with her sleeve. In weeping, both men and women wipe away their tears with their sleeves; to express worry, the character moves his hand about and contracts the forehead: in meditation, the breast is stroked with a circular motion of the hand, the finger being pointed to the temples; while to show bashfulness, the sleeve is raised before the face. Women cover their faces even more completely than male characters in order to emphasize the innate modesty of their sex. In anger, the foot is stamped, the breast pounded. When one wishes to motion a person away, the hand is waved aside or the sleeve is flourished outward, while to signal a person to come, the hand is waved up and down. To show fear, the body is turned aside and one hides. While the foregoing examples are in accordance with theatrical convention, still they are not so very far removed from the practices of everyday life. In this respect, then, Chinese drama is not unlike European drama.

PART 5
COSTUMES OF THE CHINESE STAGE

In the vernacular of the Chinese stage, wearing apparel is generally termed *hsing-t'ou* (行頭), and is designed according to strict convention. The outstanding modes of the T'ang, Sung, Yüan, and Ming dynasties supply the patterns for conventional stage clothing. No matter what character type is concerned, the clothing is designed according to a standard that grows from a combination of the modes of these various dynasties, no special attention being paid to any one dynasty or locality. A brief description of the more important garments follows:

The Robe, or *Mang*
(蟒)

The *mang* has a soft, kerchief-like collar, its large, overlapping front being buttoned from the collar, down under the arm and down the side; it also has inner (literally, "water," *shui*, 水) sleeves, which are long, flimsy, trailing silken inner sleeves, attached to the ordinary sleeves and hanging a few feet below the waist-line, almost touching the ground. The body of the robe is satin, usually embroidered with dragons; while the lower border is decorated with representations of sea-waves. This is the most important garment for official attire, and is worn in audience with the Son of Heaven, at official gatherings, at formal ceremonies, banquets, etc., or on any occasion of first importance. The colours indicate the rank of the wearer, as imperial yellow for the emperor and the crown prince, incense-brown or white for old officials, red or blue for upright persons, and black for brusque-mannered or treacherous natures. On important festive occasions, even warriors wear the *mang*. The *mang* worn by women, while in general like that worn by men, is somewhat shorter.

The Official Robe, or *Kuan I*
(官衣)

The *kuan i*, or official robe, is in general like the *mang*, just described. Previous to the Ming dynasty, officials of the highest rank only could wear the *mang*; so officials of the middle and the lower rank were obliged to wear the *kuan i*. Embroidered squares are attached to the front and back of the garment. Robes may be red, blue, or black, the rank of the official being graded in the order of the colours here mentioned. The robes of the officials of lowest rank are strikingly similar to the *mang*, except there is no embroidery, and at the opening at the sides of the *kuan i*, there is a pair of small, wing-shaped decorations projecting to the rear.

The *P'ei*
(帔)

The robe known as the *p'ei* has a large collar and buttons down the front, with long, inner sleeves, reaching almost to the knees. The material is of satin, with various decorations, the flowers being sewn on entire or in scattered blossoms or broken branches. There are also *p'ei* without embroidery. Being an important garment, it is worn in ordinary banquet scenes or at official trials. The colour and the manner of wearing this robe are similar to the *mang*. People of advanced age wear only blue or incense-brown, while those of middle age wear blue, and youth dons red. The *p'ei* worn by female characters is about the same as that worn by male characters, although young unmarried women wear a garment made of soft material, known as the *kuei mên p'ei* (閨門帔), or "maiden's gown," which is of red or pale-blue silk that may or may not be embroidered.

The Lined Coat, or *Tieh-tzŭ*
(褶子)

The lined coat, known as the *tieh-tzŭ*, buttons under the arm, and reaches to the feet. It has a large collar and inner sleeves. A woman's *tieh-tzŭ* is somewhat shorter than a man's. The garment may be soft or stiff, the former being made of soft silk, while the latter is made of stiff satin, which may or may not be embroidered. This is one of the most common garments of the stage, the plain *tieh-tzŭ* being more widely used than the embroidered one. In colouring and manner of wearing, it is, in general, like the *p'ei*. A plain blue *tieh-tzŭ* is usually associated with a young scholar, while a plain black one is worn by a poverty-stricken person. When a plain black *tieh-tzŭ* is decorated with pieces of silk of various colours to represent torn places and mending in the garment, it is worn by the poorest person and called the *fu kuei i* (富貴衣), or "garment of wealth and distinction," because the character who wears it, although very poor in the beginning, is, however, a person of lasting ambition and will surely attain high position and good fortune. There is a *tieh-tzŭ* of pure white to be worn by aged villagers, male or female, or by gods of the earth, etc., and is called a *lao tou i* (老頭衣), or "an old person's garment." The *tieh-tzŭ* may be worn by military or civil characters.

COSTUMES OF THE CHINESE STAGE

The Eunuch's Coat, or *T'ai Chien I*
(太監衣)

The *ta'i chien i* is worn exclusively by eunuchs, the garment having a large soft collar and buttoning down the side. The material may be red or brown silk, the whole having wide borders of black or blue. The waist may or may not be decorated or embroidered. The coat, reaching to the feet, has inner sleeves.

The Jade Belt, or *Yü Tai*
(玉帶)

The jade belt is considered a very important article in an actor's wardrobe. When wearing the *mang* or the *kuan i*, the jade belt is worn about the waist, this being the vogue previous to the Ming dynasty. The actual belt is made of stiff material, which is studded with pieces of jade. That worn on the stage is almost an exact replica of the real one.

The Skirt, or *Ch'ün*
(裙)

The skirt is worn exclusively by female characters. An official skirt is plaited and embroidered, but a common skirt is without decoration of any kind. Skirts of present-day style have only four panels. When a skirt is fastened well above the waist, it is an indication that the wearer is a poor woman in travelling garb, which is supposed to be disarranged.

The Jacket and Trousers, or *K'u Ao*
(褲襖)

Old stage traditions, at least, did not permit women to show their trousers; but now, for a century, the vivacious character type, known as the *hua-tan*, has always worn jacket and trousers, doing away with the skirt. The jacket has plain sleeves, without the inner sleeves, and a small collar. It is about half the length of the body, and is buttoned down the side with cord-fasteners. These characteristics, however, are entirely after the modes of the day and not according to orthodox stage tradition. Women wear such costumes on ordinary occasions only; on formal and festive occasions, they don the *p'ei*.

The Vest, or *K'an Chien*
(坎肩)

The vest is worn by maidservants only and is made of silk that may or may not be embroidered, and may or may not be bordered with other material. There are two kinds: those of knee-length follow the old convention; while the short ones, which come barely to the waist, follow, like the jacket and trousers, the modes of the day.

Costumes for Palace Women, or *Kung I*
(宮 衣)

The *kung i*, or palace garment, is worn by princesses, daughters of aristocratic families, or celestial beings, never by women of humble birth. Thus, the garment is called the palace robe. It is made of embroidered silk, having silken sashes as well as inner sleeves; and is about knee-length.

The Tasseled Cape, or *Yün Chien*
(雲 肩)

The "cloud" cape, or *yün chien*, is a most important article in a *tan's* wardrobe, and may be worn over a *mang*, a *p'ei*, or a *kung i*. Empresses, princesses, and palace women may wear this garment, which is a circular cape, embellished with tassels and embroidery. It is worn on the shoulders.

The Storm Cloak, or *Tou Fêng*
(斗 篷)

The *tou fêng*, or storm cloak, which had its origin among the Mongols of the Yüan period, was first worn, while travelling, as protection against, wind, snow, storms, etc. At home, when getting up on a cold night, it may be thrown about the shoulders; when worn on the stage it indicates that the wearer is not fully dressed. The garment has a small collar and no sleeves. Both men and women wear these cloaks ankle-length; but while men wear scarlet silk without embroidery, women may wear any colour, and use any variety of embroidery, the lower edge of the garment having, in some cases, a fringe of tassels.

A Modern *Tieh-tzŭ*, or *Shih Shih Tieh-tzŭ*
(時 式 褶 子)

The modern *tieh-tzŭ*, or lined coat, is worn by youthful women only and is made of soft silk, which may or may not be embroidered. Although it may be of any colour, a plain black one is worn by the poorest of women. This garment, which has a small collar, buttons down the front, and has inner sleeves that reach to the knees. This coat came into vogue during the first part of the Ch'ing dynasty. Recently the modern *tieh-tzŭ* has been more popular among female impersonators.

1, 2. *P'ei* (see p. 98).   3, 4. Lined Coat, or *Tieh-tzŭ* (see p. 98).   5, 6. Robe, or *Mang* (see p. 97).   7, 8. Official Robes, or *Kuan I* (see p. 97)

1. Modern, or *Shih Shih T'ieh-tzŭ* (see p. 100). 2. Jacket and Trousers, or *K'u Ao* (see p. 99). 3. Vest, or *K'an Chien* (see p. 99). 4. Storm Cloak, or *Tou Fêng* (see p. 100). 5. Palace Costume, or *Kung I* (see p. 100). 6, 7. Skirts, or *Ch'ün* (see p. 99). 8. Ancient Costume, or *Ku Chuang* (see p. 103)

1, 7, 8. Warrior's Regalia, or *K'ai K'ao* (see p. 101). 2. Regalia for Warrioress, or *Pien K'ao* (see p. 103). 3. Ordinary Official Robe, or *K'ai Ch'ang* (see p. 101). 4. Fighting Costume, or *Ta I* (see p. 102). 5. Manchu Coat, or *Ch'i I* (see p. 101). 6. Tasselled Cape, or *Yün Chien* (see p. 100); Jade Belt, or *Yü Tai* (see p. 99). 7, 8. Military Flags, or *Kao Ch'i* (see p. 101)

1. Vest for Ordinary Wear and Vest for a Monk or Priest. 2. Eight-Figured Diagram Robe, or *Pa Kua I* (see p. 103). 3. Eunuch's Coat, or *T'ai Chien I* (see p. 99). 4. Dragon Robe, or *Lung T'ao I* (see p. 103). 5. Jacket for a Military or Heroic Type. 6. Sash and Embroidered Piece Representing Armour. 7. Arrow Costume, or *Chien I* (see p. 102). 8. The Short Jacket, or *Ma Kua* (see p. 102)

COSTUMES OF THE CHINESE STAGE

The Manchu Coat, or *Ch'i I*
(旗衣)

The *ch'i i*, worn during the Ch'ing dynasty, is used by female impersonators when playing the rôles of Manchu or Mongolian women. The coat, made of embroidered silk, consists of a large collar, buttons of silk cord down the side, and wide sleeves without inner sleeves. It comes down to the feet. Sometimes, a short jacket, known as a *ma kua*, or a vest, is worn over the upper part of the gown. The *ma kua* and the vest, while similar to those of the stage, differ slightly in measurement.

Warrior's Regalia, or *K'ai K'ao*
(鎧靠)

The *k'ai k'ao* is the most important garment in a stage warrior's wardrobe, and is worn while in public service or when going to battle; but when in audience with the emperor, reviewing soldiers, or on festive occasions, a *mang* must be worn over the whole. Its colour scheme and manner of wearing are similar to those of the *mang*. An old general of distinction wears a brown *k'ai k'ao*, while a youthful warrior wears a white or a pink one. The garment, made of silk, is embroidered back and front, and has narrow sleeves. Panels, designed like armour, are added to the sides, while at the breast is the so-called "heart-protecting glass." Embroidered representations of tiger heads are attached at the waist and near the shoulders, all these details being patterned closely after ancient war regalia. The stage costume differs most largely in its more elaborate decoration and embroidery. With the exception of the many hanging streamers, or sashes, the female warrior's costume is like that of the warrior's. But only men wear the *k'ai k'ao*.

The Ordinary Official Robe, or *K'ai Ch'ang*
(開氅)

The *k'ai ch'ang* is a robe also worn by military officials, but since it is not so important as the *k'ai k'ao*, it may be worn on informal occasions, as well as at the meetings of higher officers. Its colour scheme and the manner of wearing it are similar to the *k'ai k'ao*. The *k'ai ch'ang* has a large collar, buttons down the side, and has inner sleeves. The entire robe is embroidered, while from the openings under the arms protrude a pair of wing-shaped objects. The garment, reaching to the feet, is worn by warriors only.

Military Flags, or *K'ao Ch'i*
(靠旗)

The *k'ao ch'i* are simply the flags worn on a warrior's back when he enters the fray. The origin of these flags grew from their actual use by a general, who, when issuing orders in the thick of battle, gave one of his subordinates a flag to serve as a warrant. On one side of the flag were marks of identity. Every general took with him one or two flags to be used in cases of emergency. Thus the flags now included in the stage regalias of generals still retain the old idea of field orders; but the fact that there are four flags is due to the desire for a beautiful effect. The flags, triangular in form, are made of silk and embroidered with flowers or dragons. Their colour should be the same as that of the warrior's robe — as, white flags for a white robe, black for a black one, etc.

The Fighting Costume, or *Ta I*
(打衣)

The *ta i* is worn for unofficial struggles, private fights, expeditions to capture robbers, or mêlées between supernatural beings. When there is a hot contest between common soldiers, drawn up face to face, this costume is often used; it is understood that the battle is not official and not fought for the nation. If, however, the empire has a female general, she may wear such garments, which consist of a short jacket with a large or small collar, with buttons down the side or down the front. The large collar, however, was used in the old drama, while the small collar was introduced later. The lower hem of the jacket reaches to the waist-line or a trifle below. The sleeves are tight, and the garment may or may not be embroidered. The trousers, like those worn in real life, may or may not be embroidered.

The Arrow Costume, or *Chien I*
(箭衣)

The *chien i*, or arrow costume, which is worn by generals in the thick of battle, did not, however, have a place in the old drama; it was introduced during the Ch'ing dynasty. The garment has a small collar, silk cord buttons that fasten down the side, and narrow sleeves, which open in the shape of a horseshoe. The garment reaches to the feet. The robe, decorated with dragons, is embroidered at its lower border with representations of sea waves; hence these are called "dragon-arrow robes," while the unembroidered garments are called "plain-arrow robes." The *chien i*, always worn with a phœnix belt or with hanging sashes, was, during the Ch'ing period, the regulation costume for archers; hence its name.

The Short Jacket, or *Ma Kua*
(馬掛)

The *ma kua* is a garment still worn in everyday life, and is indispensable on formal occasions. Invariably of black silk, a *ma kua* buttons down the front and reaches a bit below the waist-line. On the stage, the garment may be the semi-official garb of emperor or general, travelling on the road. The emperor alone is privileged to wear a *ma kua* of deep yellow, while all others wear black. Embroidered dragons are a common decoration. The stage *ma kua*, having a small collar and buttoning down the front, was also introduced during the late Ch'ing dynasty.

The Glass Abdomen, or *Pien K'ao*
(玻璃肚子；便靠)

The *pien k'ao* is the exclusive robe for female warriors, and is devoid of all cloth streamers or sashes. While in general its measurements correspond to those of a male warrior's costume, the female warrior, when wearing this garment, never has flags attached to the shoulders.

The Eight-Figured Diagram Robe, or *Pa Kua I*
(八卦衣)

The *pa kua i* is, in reality, a *p'ei*, which, instead of the customary embroidery, has for decoration the Taoist eight-figured diagram. This wide-bordered garment is worn exclusively by Taoists, blue, purple, etc., being popular colours on the stage. Advisers to generals always study Taoism in order to become masters of astronomy, geography, etc. All magic centers about the *pa kua*.

The Dragon Robe, or *Lung T'ao I*
(龍套衣)

It was the custom, in ancient Chinese warfare, when the spears and swords of opposing sides had been crossed for battle, for the greater and lesser generals to do battle while the common soldiery merely stood in position, prepared to ward off a possible charge on the part of the enemy. Hence they did not battle at the time, but waited for their leaders to win, thereafter charging and finally doing battle among themselves. This, then, is the actual method of procedure in ancient warfare. The soldiers, who, in the drama, make such a battle formation, wear long robes and carry banners, while standing to either side of the stage, never fighting. In a play, four or eight such super-numeraries may represent scores, hundreds, and even thousands of common soldiery. The dragon robe has a round collar, buttons down the front, and has embroidered dragons, with representations of sea-waves. The colours are many, the colour of the flag being the same as that of the robe. The garment, having long inner sleeves, reaches almost to the wearer's feet.

The Ancient Costume, or *Ku Chuang*
(古裝)

What is known as the *ku chuang*, or ancient costume, was the habit of the women of two thousand years ago. In the strict sense of the word, Chinese drama, in times past, had no historically correct costume of this type; furthermore, the details of the costume had well-nigh been lost, and what examples were extant could be seen on old paintings only. Within a decade, Mr. Mei Lan-fang, having spent much time in reclaiming the details of this dress, was finally able to assemble an ancient costume for use in theatres. Now, "like the wind," it is current throughout the length and breadth of China. The styles, created and reclaimed by Mei, are too numerous to describe here.

Animal Costumes, or *Shou I*
(獸衣)

When a cow, a horse, a tiger, or a wolf are to be represented, the actor wears a cloth costume, fashioned in form after the animal to be imitated so that the spectator may, at one glance, see which animal is meant.

Weeds of Mourning, or *Shang Fu I*
(喪服衣)

As in real life, the mourning clothes of the stage are white; thus, in drama, the actor may wear white silk or cloth. A plain hat or one with a white band tied to the side, as a mark of recent bereavement, may be worn, while, at times, the hair is purposely dishevelled in order to indicate frenzied grief. Garments of coarse flax may also be worn, on occasion, to show deep mourning, as is also done in real life.

PART 6

HEADGEAR AND FOOTWEAR

The hat, the helmet, and the shoes worn in Chinese drama have been designed from a combination of the styles that prevailed during the T'ang, Sung, Yüan, and Ming dynasties, and bear a very close resemblance to the originals, although those used on the stage are somewhat more elaborate. The more important kinds of headgear and footwear will be considered as follows:

The Helmet or Hat, or K'uei

(盔)

The *k'uei*, or *kuan*, is the most important hat of officialdom, the emperor and high military officials only being allowed to wear it. The hat of the emperor differs from all others in that it is studded with pearls which take the form of a phœnix, the emblem of royalty. Tassels hang from the sides. While the hat worn by military officials is somewhat like that of the emperor's, yet the form varies according to the rank of the person in question. For instance, a robber chief may wear a hat that is shaped only a trifle differently from that of the emperor.

The Gauze Hat, or *Sha Mao*

(紗帽)

The *sha mao*, or gauze hat, also for officials, is worn exclusively by civil dignitaries when waiting on the emperor, attending public trials, or at important festivities and banquets. Its form is very much like that used in real life: low in front, high at the back, and black in colour. Horizontally from the sides extend a pair of wing-shaped decorations. Officials of highest rank may wear a long, narrow decoration that is slightly curved in the middle; the next in rank may wear oval-shaped ones; a rank lower may wear round ones; while the official of lowest rank wears round decorations that are pointed on the outer sides.

APPENDIX

The Soft Hat, or *Chin*
(巾)

The *chin*, a hat for ordinary wear, is different from the *k'uei* (helmet) and the *mao* (hat); for the latter are made of stiff material, while the former is made of soft cloth or felt. There is, however, such a bewildering variety of *chin*, or soft hats, as to defy description; it is sufficient to point out that the soft hats worn in Chinese drama are technically known as *chin*.

The Military Hat, or *Lo Mao*
(羅帽)

The *lo mao* is also worn by military persons and it finds its origin in the pages of history, although the stage hat has undergone marked changes. In form, it is large at the top and small near the head, while its six sides are richly embroidered and decorated with pearls and jade, its top being adorned with fluffy silken balls of various colours. This lavish display has for its sole purpose the pleasing of the eye.

The Phœnix Hat, or *Fêng Kuan*
(鳳冠)

Although the *fêng kuan*, or phœnix hat, is worn exclusively by women on formal occasions, yet only empresses, princesses, and women of high official families are privileged to wear such headgear. They consist of a framework, thickly studded with pearls and jade, from the sides of which depend tassels, while other tassels cover the forehead.

The Wind Hat, or *Fêng Mao*
(風帽)

The *fêng mao*, or wind hat, is used as protection against wind- and snow-storms and may be worn while travelling, or when one first gets up at night. It is similar in use to the *tou fêng*. The wind hat is made of red satin, and may or may not be embroidered. Placed on the head, it hangs a few feet below the head.

Pheasant Plumes, or *Chih Wei*
(雉尾)

The *chih wei* are the two long pheasant plumes that are attached to the actor's headgear, the longest specimens being as much as six or seven feet in length. Such feathers indicate that the wearer is a barbarian; hence, those impersonating robber chiefs, or military leaders of Mongolia or other barbarian regions, use such plumes. As time

HEADGEAR

1. Styles in Soft Hats, or *Chin* (see p. 106)
2. Styles in Stiff Hats, or *K'uei* (see p. 105)
3. Phœnix Hat, or *Fêng Kuan* (see p. 106)
4. Hats, or *Mao* (see p. 106)
5. Imperial Hat
6. Wig for a Child

HEADGEAR AND FOOTWEAR

passed, stage characters in the rôles of Chinese generals, because of their beauty also wore the *chih wei*; but this is a violation of orthodox theatrical convention. Generally speaking, the plumes are worn by officials or warriors who are not fighting for China. While youthful Chinese stage generals are fond of wearing the pheasant plumes, because of their pleasing appearance, there is no justification for such a practice.

Fox-Tails, or *Hu Wei*
(狐 尾)

The *hu wei*, or fox-tails, are the two long, white, fluffy fur strands that hang from the head-dress of a barbarian general; they are worn by military officers, and usually, when not in battle, hang over the breast; but as soon as the warrior enters the fray, the fox-tails are thrown back over the shoulders. Similar in use to the pheasant plumes, the fox-tails denote that the wearer is a barbarian.

Shoes and Boots, or *Hsüeh Hsieh*
(靴 鞋)

Every one in ancient China, from the emperor to the scholar and merchant, wore shoes; actors wear the same, the only exception being those playing the parts of laborers and farmers. While stage footwear is generally like that worn in everyday life, the soles of the former are a trifle thicker in order to give the actor additional height. Women wear shoes that are usually embroidered, while warriors' boots are embroidered and thin-soled. The embroidery is merely to please the eye.

PART 7

BEARDS AND MOUSTACHES, OR *HU HSÜ*
(鬍鬚)

Since the ancients of China prized a long beard most of all, it came about that actors wore long, artificial beards. Although at first beards were not so long as those at present, yet afterwards the stage beard gradually increased in length. Varying through shades of white and black, the beard may indicate the age of the wearer. Red or blue beards are worn by people of questionable character, masters of black magic, or supernatural beings, and are made of horse-hair.

The Full Beard, or *Man Jan*
(滿髯)

A full beard, which covers the mouth, indicates that the owner is both wealthy and heroic.

The Tripart Beard, or *San Jan*
(三髯)

A beard divided into three parts shows that the wearer is a person of culture and refinement.

The Short Moustache, or *Tuan Jan*
(短髯)

The short moustache, only an inch in length, indicates a rude and unrefined person.

Miscellaneous Remarks

The types of beards are too numerous to consider in detail. Briefly, it may be said that a moustache which points upward reveals a crafty nature, one that droops downward indicates a dirty or uncouth person, while some beards are worn merely to win laughs from the spectators, etc., ad infinitum.

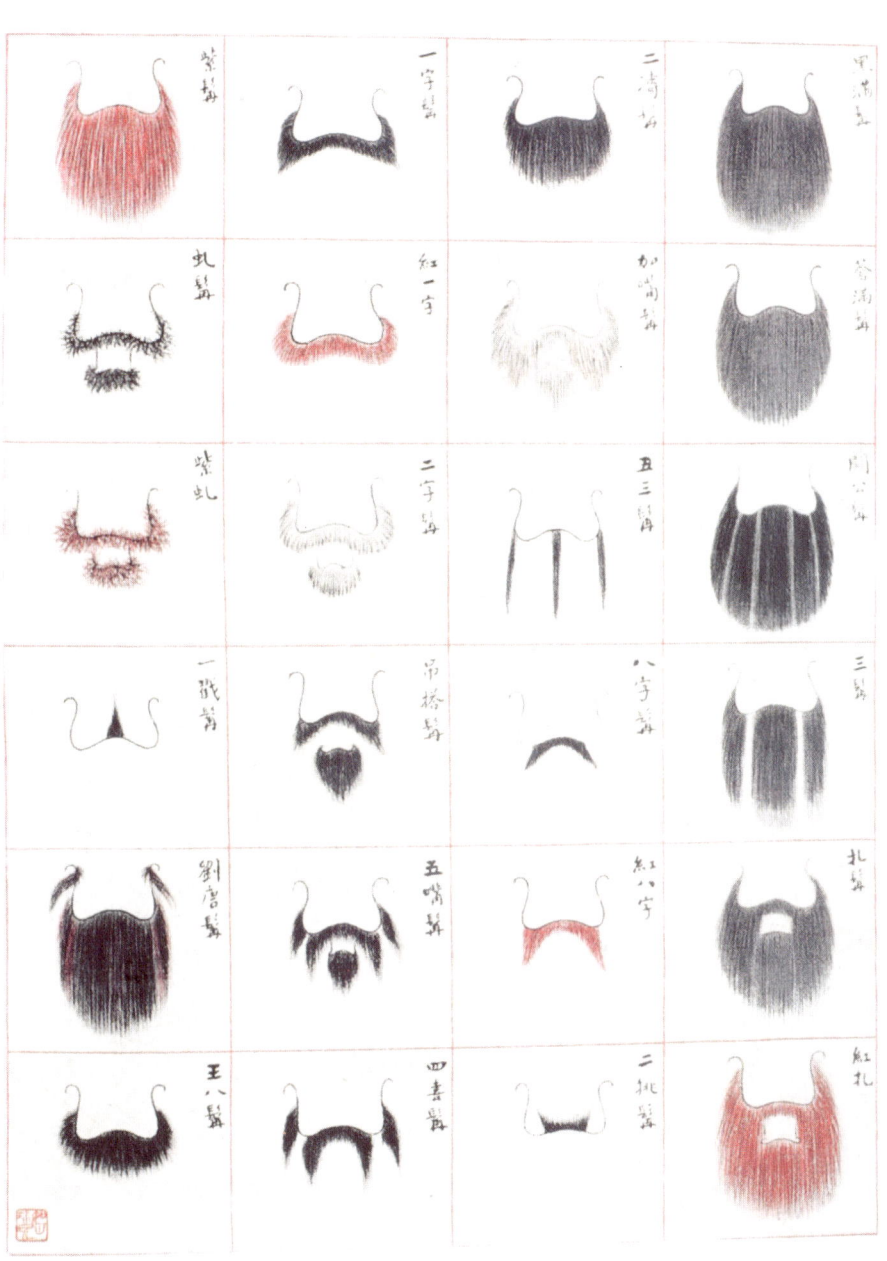

BEARDS
For Full Beards, or *Man Jan*, and Tripart Beards, or *San Jan*, see page 108.

BEARDS AND MOUSTACHES

Note. In the original Chinese manuscript, a very short article on the art of facial painting appeared at this point. Mr. Chao Suh-yong, who in most matters represents Mr. Mei Lan-fang in Shanghai, requested that this part be transposed to Part I of the Appendix. On page 82 these three short paragraphs appear under the heading "The Characters with Painted Faces, or *Ching*." The Chinese of the first paragraph is written by Mr. Chao.

PART 8

STAGE PROPERTIES AND SYMBOLISM

Since in the old drama every situation, every object, must be abstract in nature and often symbolical, pure realism is invariably shunned and realistic stage properties are not favoured. In the gags and bickerings of the comedians, however, realism may be found; but the ohter important members of the cast are not permitted liberties of speech and action. Every object on the stage is fashioned according to strict convention. Sometimes a common object may be symbolized, as, for instance, an oar may represent a boat. The following examples make this clear:

The Horse-Whip, or *Ma Pien*
(馬 鞭)

Symbolism on the Chinese stage allows the holding of a whip by an actor to indicate that he is on a horse. Both the mounting and the dismounting of a horse are represented by strict conventional pantomimic movements. If one has already dismounted from the unseen horse, he may still hold the whip; but in such a case, the whip must be allowed to hang at the rider's side. When one is about to fasten a horse to a post or a tree, he need only place the whip on the ground or hand the same to another person who is supposed to lead the animal away. A brown whip represents a brown horse; black, white, or reddish whips stand for horses of corresponding colour. But when a whip is decorated with a bewildering variety of colours, it must be confessed that there is no such horse; it is merely a desire to please the eye!

Wagon Flags, or *Ch'ê Ch'i*
(車 旗)

A wagon or a wheelbarrow is represented by two flags, on each of which is painted a wheel. On the stage, with the exception of Chu-ko Liang and one or two other male characters, the occupants of this flimsy representation of a wagon are women exclusively. The novel of the "Three Kingdoms" makes it clear that the great strategist, Chu-ko Liang, rode in a wagon, as do civil officials and other non-military officers, because

STAGE PROPERTIES AND SYMBOLISM

they were believed to be poor horsemen. The flags are manipulated as follows: a servant holds the handles of the two flags, between which the occupant stands or walks. Definite pantomime shows that one has entered or stepped out of the wagon. Strict convention demands that the wagon come on the stage as soon as it is needed and that it go off the stage as soon as the rider has stepped out, because the flags must never be set down on the stage.

The Sedan, or *Chiao-tzŭ*
(轎子)

The most unsubstantial and most highly conventionalized object on the Chinese stage is a sedan chair. While in horse riding there is a whip to hold and in wagon riding there are two flags to be seen, the sedan is represented by nothing except thin air! One who wishes to indicate that he has entered a sedan, merely bends the body, moving backwards, while two attendants move their hands as if letting down the curtains. On leaving the sedan, one lifts the imaginary curtains and departs.

The Duster, or *Ying Ch'ên*
(蠅麈)

The symbol of greatest refinement and the most highly treasured object throughout the long centuries of Chinese history is the duster of horse-hair. The *literati*, while conversing, delight in fingering it; thus, in Chinese drama, only the most exalted persons may hold a duster, such as gods, demigods, bodhisattvas, Buddhist monks, Taoist priests, wanderers, recluses, celestial beings, and spirits of many orders. Sometimes, however, a maidservant may use a duster to clean the furniture. In general, then, a duster is very common in the Chinese drama and may represent any number of things.

The Cloth City Wall, or *Pu Ch'êng*
(布城)

The stage city wall consists of blue cloth, on which are painted white lines to represent bricks in order to give a resemblance to an old wall. Whenever the text of the play calls for a wall, two attendants, lifting a cloth representation of the structure, take their place on the stage. Since the arch is often too low, the attendants, who have nothing to do with the play, elevate the cloth gate in order to facilitate the passage of those who enter or leave the city. Although this is a very simple piece of stage property, it is practically the sole genuine bit of scenery in Chinese drama.

APPENDIX

Wind Flags, or *Fêng Ch'i*
(風旗)

When the text requires a great wind, four black flags, called wind flags, are carried and waved about by four attendants, who rush by to show that spirits are "riding on the wind."

Water Flags, or *Shui Ch'i*
(水旗)

Four flags, with sea billows painted on a white surface to represent ocean waves, are used to represent water, as when a character leaps into a river and is rescued. Such flags are carried across the stage by four attendants.

The Great Curtain, or *Ta Chang-tzŭ*
(大帳子)

The *ta chang-tzŭ* is a large, embroidered curtain, which may be used for many settings, most of them being associated with women, some of which are as follows: a bed, a canopy, or a bright tower. When a generalissimo assumes his post or an official of high rank sits in state, the great curtain is also used; in no case may it be hung when minor officials are in session. On the other hand, the emperor seldom makes use of this hanging, while the empress dowager invariably does. In the last use, the curtain represents the imperial curtain, from behind which the empress dowager gave audience.

Mountain Rocks, or *Shan Shih P'ien*
(山石片)

Cloth nailed to oblong wooden frames on which are painted representations of mountain rocks are used in Chinese drama to show that the characters have arrived in a hilly region. When one is to ascend a mountain, these blocks of "mountain" are placed in front of the actors in order to represent a mountain range. For this purpose two or four blocks are sufficient; if one is to go through a mountain pass, one or two blocks may be placed on either side of the path before the travellers to represent the rocky formations that tower to either side. This, then, is also a genuine example of scenery in the older drama.

The Table, or *Cho-tzŭ*
(桌子)

The *cho-tzŭ*, or table, represents, perhaps, more things than any other single object, some of them being as follows: a teapoy, a dining table, a judge's desk, an incense

STAGE PROPERTIES AND SYMBOLISM

table, etc.; while the acts of going from lower to higher levels, as the ascent of a mountain or the scaling of a wall, may also be effected by using a table. When in actual use, the table may be placed in an ordinary position, on its side, etc., or in any manner which is appropriate to the scene. There is no fixed rule for such placing.

The Chair, or *I-tzŭ*
(椅子)

Although the chair is the most common object used for sitting, yet the manner in which a chair is placed on the stage makes a decided difference. If one is sitting in a palace, at an official gathering, or while reading or writing, the *i-tzŭ*, or chair, is placed behind the table and then it is called a *nei chang i-tzŭ* (內塲椅子), or a "chair inside." If one is making preparations to receive guests, relatives, etc., for a quiet chat, then the chair is placed in front of the table and is called a *wai chang i-tzŭ* (外塲椅子), or a "chair outside." There are, however, certain important occasions when a chair is placed behind the table. Hair-splitting distinctions as to the manner of placing a *wai chang i-tzŭ* exist. For example, the parents are seated in the centre, the place of honour, while the children take seats to the sides. Host and guest of equal rank sit to either side of the table in the centre of the stage, those of lower rank seating themselves farther away from the centre. On some occasions, women sit to the right side and men to the left, the latter being the side of honour. If a father and a mother are seated, the daughter unfailingly takes the seat to the right, while the son takes the seat to the left. The manner of seating just described is that followed in daily life. If, however, an actor is supposed to be sitting on the ground, on rocks, or in any other unconventional position, the chair is placed on its side to describe such a position, this being called a *tao-i* (倒椅), or a "chair on its side." If a female character must climb to a high place, she uses a chair to represent the eminence. Although a male character may, at times, use a chair for the same purpose, he prefers a table for such a situation. Again, two or three chairs placed together may represent a bed, while a cloak or large covering is placed over the whole to complete the representation.

The Mandate Arrow, or *Ling Chien*
(令箭)

Whenever the generals of old issued military orders, these were accompanied by an arrow, which served as proof of the order's authenticity; there was also the idea that the order must proceed as swiftly as an arrow. Thus it has come about in the drama that both military and civil officers use the *ling chien*, or mandate arrow, to send off orders, the only difference being that the stage arrow is larger than that used in actual life. The stage arrow is also more elaborate and is not too faithful a reproduction of the former, because actors fear to displease officialdom by imitating too faithfully anything the latter uses.

APPENDIX

The Standard, or *Fu Chieh*
(符 節)

The *fu chieh* is a kind of decorative standard, having at one end the representation of a dragon's head, or some other figure; while from the long, crooked shaft depends a cord, which supports four or five rows of tassels. Emperors, empresses, princesses, the queen of the fairies, etc., on coming upon the stage, are preceded by attendants carrying a pair of these standards, which indicate that the person has important official business or is coming with important property or letters. These *fu chieh* accompany him both as credentials and as a protection, at the same time emphasizing the full extent of that personage's rank. Thus the emperor and empress, whenever going abroad, carried before them the *fu chieh*. Those of the stage, because of a desire for the spectacular, are slightly more decorative than the actual standards.

The Long-Handled Fan, or *Chang Shan*
(掌 扇)

The *chang shan*, or long-handled fan, used for shelter from the heat of the sun or for fanning, may be found in the palaces of almost every oriental nation, because of the intense heat. When an emperor, an empress, or a princess goes out in the open, two attendants unfailingly carry behind such personages a pair of long-handled fans. The queen of the fairies may also use these fans, which merely indicate the importance of the person in question. The fan, or *shan*, may be made of feathers or of embroidered silk, but the prerequisite is the long handle. The stage fan is not unlike that used in actual life.

The Umbrella, or *San*
(傘)

The *san*, or umbrella, employed for protection from sun and rain, is commonly used in the orient. A *san* is held from behind, over the head of the emperor and empress whenever they go abroad. When officials conduct their business in the open, they also use the umbrella, while the fairies include pretty umbrellas in their train in order to appeal to the audience's sense of beauty. *San* are made of silk, plain or embroidered, and the handles may be straight or curved, but are always long. The curved handles give the character more prestige than the straight ones.

The Lantern, or *Têng*
(燈)

The emperor, the empress, the female relatives of the emperor, and other members of the royal palace, when going about at night, were accustomed to carry before

1. Flag, or *Mên Ch'iang Ch'i* (see p. 115). 2. Banner of a Generalissimo
3, 4. Umbrellas, or *San* (see p. 114). 5. Cloth City Wall, or *Pu Ch'ên*
(see p. 111). 6. Great Curtain, or *Ta Chang-tzǔ* (see p. 112). 7. Mountai
Rocks, or *Shan Shih P'ien* (see p. 112). 8. Flag of a General

1. Mandate Arrow, or *Ling Chien* (see p. 113). 2. Imperial Mandate. 3. Lantern, or *Têng* (see p. 114). 4. Table, or *Cho-tzŭ* (see p. 112). 5. Chair, or *I-tzŭ* (see p. 113). 6. Bench. 7. Long-Handled Fan, or *Chang Shan* (see p. 114). 8. Lantern, or *Têng* (see p. 114). 9. Oar. 10. Tablet, or *Hu* (see p. 115). 11. Duster, or *Ying Ch'ên* (see p. 111). 12. Whip, or *Ma Pien* (see p. 110). 13. Wagon Flag, or *Ch'ê Ch'i* (see p. 110). 14. Wind Flag, or *Fêng Ch'i* (see p. 112). 15. Water Flag, or *Shui Ch'i* (see p. 112). 16, 17. Imperial Standards. 18. Standard, or *Fu Chieh* (see p. 114). 19. Umbrella, or *San* (see p. 114). 20, 21, 22, 23, 24. Banners and Flags.

STAGE PROPERTIES AND SYMBOLISM

them several pairs of lanterns; thus, for similar scenes in the drama, lanterns are also used. They may be made of glass, decorated with fringes, or of gauze, edged with tassels, and are held by wooden handles. Officials going about at night also have lanterns of ordinary size carried before them.

The Ivory Tablet, or *Hu*
(牙笏)

The ivory *hu* was used by officials, civil and military, previous to the Ming dynasty, as a mark of respect to the reigning house, and also as a means of making memoranda which later might be reported to the emperor. In the drama, when an official has audience with the emperor, he must hold a *hu*, which is usually made of ivory and is a foot or more long and two inches wide, being narrow at the top and wide at the bottom.

Miscellaneous Objects

Pens, ink slabs, cups, teapots, lamps, books, writing paraphernalia, legal documents, boxes, and cans, as well as all manner of small objects, are made entirely of wood.

Stage Clouds, or *Yün P'ien*
(雲片)

Because celestial beings, when they move about, are sure to disturb the elements as they pass through the atmosphere, four "cloud children," or attendants, each holding a painted representation of a cloud, walk across the stage to represent such a situation. These "clouds" may be made of heavy cardboard or of cloth cut to resemble real clouds, while paint is applied to make the likeness even more close. At other times, for the sake of the spectacular, clouds may be made in the form of a lantern; but in such a case, there is no additional significance.

The Flag on Top of a Soldier's Spear, or *Mên Ch'iang Ch'i*
(門槍旗)

The *mên ch'iang ch'i* is the flag at the top of an ordinary soldier's spear, ostensibly to ward off enemy arrows. The flags are of different colours, so that the various divisions may be the more easily discerned in battle. Red, yellow, black, white, and blue are most popular. The colours should match the robes of the generals for whom they are carried, as white *mên ch'iang ch'i* for a white robed general, etc. The flags may be of silk, embroidered with dragons and edged with red or blue borders, their length being about five feet and their width a foot or more.

116 APPENDIX

Military Weapons, or *Ping Ch'i*
(兵 器)

All military weapons used on the stage, such as lances, swords, guns, poles, etc., are made of wood, and are close likenesses of the real articles, although they may differ in measurements. Since the stage traditions do not permit the use of real weapons, wooden ones are used in the plays.

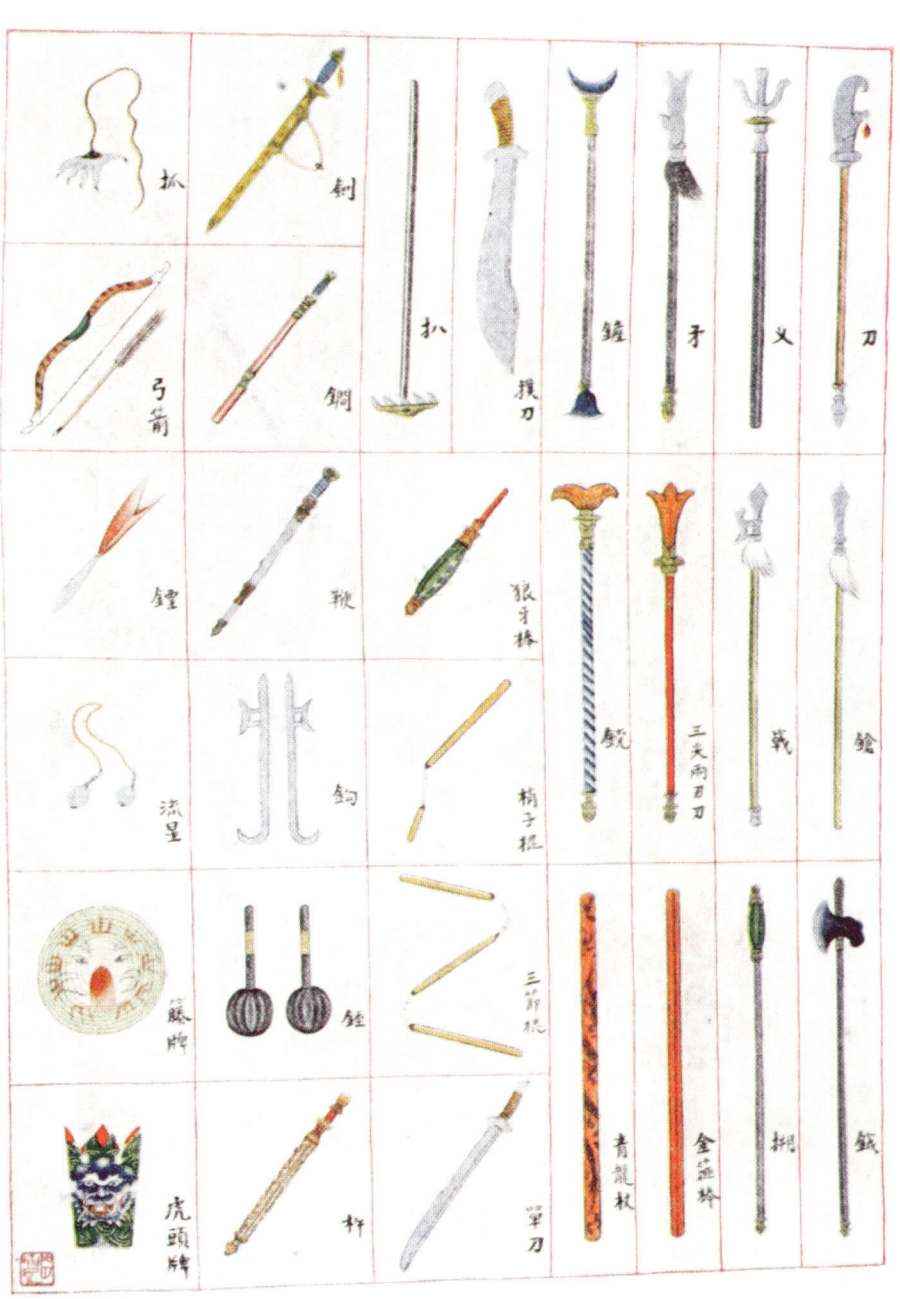

Stage Weapons (see p. 116)

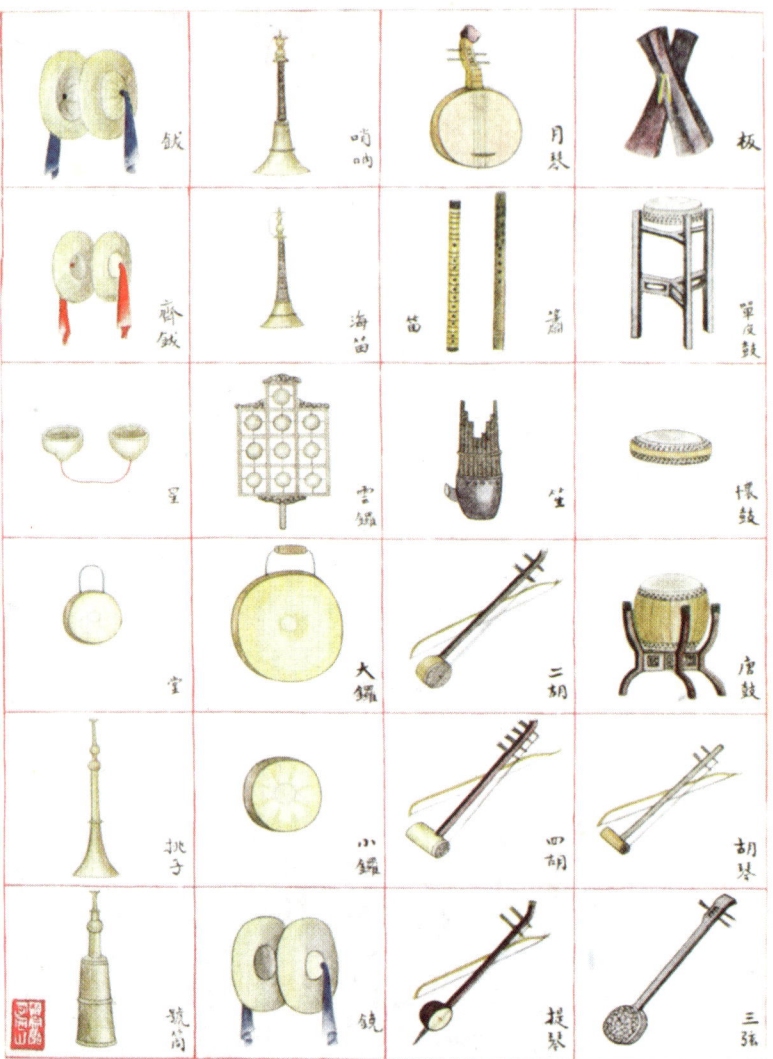

MUSICAL INSTRUMENTS

1, 2, 12. Cymbals, or *Nao* (see p. 120). 3. Bells, or *P'êng Chung* (see p. 120). 4. Gong, or *Lo* (see p. 120). 5. *T'iao-tzŭ*, Used to Represent Neighing of Horses. 6. *Hao T'ung*, Used on Entry of a General. 7. Clarinet, or *So Na* (see p. 119). 8. "Ocean" Flute, or *Hai Ti*. 9. Nine-Toned Gongs, or *Chiu Yin Lo* (see p. 121). 10. Big Gong, or *Ta Lo* (see p. 120). 11. Small Gong, or *Hsiao Lo* (see p. 120). 13. Moon Guitar, or *Yüeh-ch'in* (see p. 118). 14. *Hsiao*, Blown Vertically; Flute, or *Ti-tzŭ* (see p. 117). 15. Reed Organ, or *Shêng* (see p. 119). 16. Two-Stringed Hu, or *Erh-hu* (see p. 119). 17. Four-Stringed Hu, or *Ssŭ-hu* (see p. 119). 18. Violin with a Cocoanut Sounding-Box, or *Ti-ch'in*. 19. Wooden Time Beater, or *Pan* (see p. 117). 20. Small Drum, or *Hsiao Ku* (see p. 117). 21. Drum Used in a *K'un-ch'ü* Orchestra. 22. Great Drum, or *Ta Ku* (see p. 118). 23. Two-Stringed Chinese Violin, or *Hu-ch'in* (see p. 118). 24. Three-Stringed Guitar, or *Hsien-tzŭ* (see p. 61).

PART 9

MUSICAL INSTRUMENTS

In musical drama the world over, it is customary for instruments to accompany the voice; in Chinese drama, apart from vocal accompaniment, orchestral instruments play interpolated passages, technically known as *kuo mên* (過門), or "passing the door" as, for instance, when an actor has completed the singing of a phrase and the instruments play a few additional measures. When half a passage has been sung, instruments may also play a passage, giving the singer an opportunity to rest. In a Chinese orchestra, there are modulations of tone, pauses, and the rudiments of harmony. Although in European drama there is no *kuo mên*, certain musical passages are similar to this Chinese musical practice.

A general description of instruments follows:

The Wooden Time Beater, or *Pan*
(板)

The *pan*, or "board," is the main instrument in an orchestra for beating time. While the music of every nation pays due regard to tempo, European musicians "watch time," and Chinese instrumentalists "listen to time"; for the European conductor uses a baton to direct his musicians, while the Chinese player listens to the sound of the *pan* in order to have the instruments play in unison. The *pan* is made of three pieces of wood of the hardest variety, two of them being fastened together side by side; while the other piece is tied at one end with a cord to the others, and, when keeping time, is manipulated by one hand in such a way as to hit against the other two with a loud, resonant sound.

The Small Drum, or *Hsiao Ku*
(小鼓)

It is necessary in Chinese music to listen to the *pan*, which maintains the tempo, but at times the sound of the other music is so loud that the *pan* cannot be heard. To avoid possible confusion, the *hsiao ku*, or small drum, is used, for its sound is much louder than that of the *pan*. The *hsiao ku* gives additional indications of tempo, because sometimes the beat of the *pan* is so rare that the tempo may be lost. So, between the beats of the *pan*, drum beats, known in the stage vernacular as "auxiliary beats," are interpolated when cymbals and similar instruments are used, the small drum not only helping to beat the time, but also creating such flourishes as delight the ear. The *hsiao ku* is made of heavy circles of wood, over which is stretched thick pigskin.

The Great Drum, or *Ta Ku*
(大鼓)

The great drum is used exclusively to assist in creating the effects produced by other instruments. Except in one or two dramas only, it has no place as a solo instrument. It is made of a wooden frame, over which cow-hide is drawn. It is about the size of a European drum, but it has a much deeper resonance.

The Chinese Violin, or *Hu-ch'in*
(胡琴)

In the current *p'i-huang* drama, the *hu-ch'in*, often called the Chinese violin, is the leading instrument of vocal accompaniment. Its sound box is made of bamboo, the ends of which are covered which snake-skin, while two strings, about a foot in length, are played with a bow. The *hu-ch'in* was not originally a Chinese instrument, but came from the northern barbarian tribes, known as the *Hu*, from which it derived its name. In the course of time, however, the Chinese kept modifying the instrument, until it acquired its present form. While the *hu-ch'in* was introduced by the Ch'ings, it had been in use among the northern Hus for some time.

The Moon Guitar, or *Yüeh-ch'in*
(月琴)

The *yüeh-ch'in*, often called the Chinese guitar, is also an important instrument for vocal accompaniment, and is used to support the *hu-ch'in*. The instrument consists of a piece of round wood, with four strings, which are shorter than those of the *hu-ch'in*, being about five or six inches in length.

The Three-Stringed Guitar, or *Hsien-tzŭ*
(絃子)

The *hsien-tzŭ* is another stringed instrument that is commonly used in vocal accompaniment to assist the *hu-ch'in*. It is constructed of circular pieces of hard wood, over which snake-skin is stretched. It has three strings, about three feet in length, and possesses a slight overtone.

MUSICAL INSTRUMENTS

The Flute, or *Ti-tzŭ*
(笛 子)

The Chinese *ti-tzŭ*, also an instrument for vocal accompaniment, is considered most pleasant to the ear. It is made of a bamboo tube that is pierced with eight holes and at its second hole there is a thin layer of rush tissue. It is somewhat similar to the European flute, but is held parallel to the mouth when played. It is the leading instrument for vocal accompaniment in *kun-ch'ü* drama, and it held the most important position in the orchestra until the *hu-ch'in*, along with the *p'i-huang* drama, was introduced from the North.

The Reed Organ, or *Shêng*
(笙)

The *shêng*, also an instrument for vocal accompaniment, may be classified in the same family as the *ti-tzŭ*, or flute. While all other instruments in China are single-toned, the *shêng* alone has harmony. It is constructed of over ten pieces of bamboo, each of which contains a hole, the entire number being fastened to a frame. The sound produced by blowing, while weak, is delightful to the ear.

The Two-Stringed *Hu*, or *Êrh-Hu*
(二 胡)

The *êrh-hu*, also a stringed instrument for vocal accompaniment, possesses tones that are somewhat lower than those of the *hu-ch'in*. Like the latter instrument, it is constructed of a wooden frame, over the ends of which snake-skin is stretched, its two strings being about one foot and five inches in length. The *êrh-hu* is a modification of the *hu-ch'in*.

The Four-Stringed *Hu*, or *Ssŭ-Hu*
(四 胡)

The *ssŭ-hu* is similar in construction to the *êrh-hu*, the only difference being that it has four strings instead of two. It is an offspring of the parent *hu-ch'in*, and is also an instrument for vocal accompaniment.

The Clarinet, or *So Na*
(唢 呐)

The *so na*, while customarily used as a solo instrument, may sometimes be played for vocal accompaniment. A female impersonator never uses this instrument for singing. The *so na*, said to have been introduced from the savage tribes of the west, is made of a piece of wood, pierced with eight holes. At the upper end is a piece of rush tissue attached to the mouthpiece, producing a loud sound when blown. At the lower end is a brass sound-magnifier. The Chinese *so na* is like that of India.

The Gong, or *Lo*
(鑼)

The *lo* is an auxiliary instrument entirely, and is beaten when a musical passage is to begin or just about to close; or at times it may be sounded once or twice in the course of a musical selection, ostensibly to delight the ear. When an actor first comes upon the stage, or is about to depart, or is executing pantomimic gesture, the gong is commonly used. This instrument is made of a piece of brass, the edges of which are bent into a circle; it is struck with a wooden stick.

Cymbals, or *Nao*
(鐃)

The *nao*, or cymbals, are used after the fashion of the gong; they are also constructed of brass, the two pieces having between them a place for the hands. During the last decade, the military bands of many countries have added the *nao* to their collection of instruments.

The Small Gong, or *Hsiao Lo*
(小鑼)

The *hsiao lo*, or small gong, is similar to the large gong, and is beaten alternately with the larger instrument. It is used most when a *tan*, or female impersonator, steps upon the stage for the first time. While similar to the large gong in construction, the small gong is but six or seven inches in diameter; it is convex.

The Bell, or *P'êng Chung*
(碰鐘)

The *p'êng chung* is used exclusively to aid in keeping time, while additional tappings are made on the same to delight the ear. It is made of brass into a cup-shaped instrument, while at the upper end a hole is bored, through which a string is passed for hanging. When in use, the bells are beaten together.

MUSICAL INSTRUMENTS

The Nine-Toned Gong, or *Chiu Yin Lo*
(九音鑼)

The *chiu yin lo* is played to restricted tempo, and while used with other instruments is never sounded when an actor sings; for it is believed that the tones of this instrument confuse the tones of the human voice. The *chiu yin lo* consists of ten gong-shaped pieces of brass, each of about two inches in diameter, which are hung in a wooden frame, there being actually nine tones only, because one bell is an octave higher than the first. They are hit with a small wooden stick in strict time with the directions given in the musical score.

INDEX

INDEX

Actors
    address of welcome to Japanese by Mei Lan-fang, 60
    mixed companies of Chinese, 18
Actress, the Chinese
    brief history of, from *Asia*, 17, 18
    portrayal of male characters by, 18
    widely advertised in Peking, 18
Aside, the, originally included the soliloquy, 91
Audience, a Chinese, 27, 28
    demand quality and variety, 40
    love of, for song, 40

Beards and moustaches, or *hu hsü*, 108, 109. See Stage the, Chinese
Birth, the, of Mei Lan-fang, 11

Characters with painted faces, 109
Chêng-tan, or *ch'ing-i*, 20
    types represented by, 21, 22
Chinese, the
    Changing, The, 17
    transition period in history of, 17
Ch'ing-i, model of correct behaviour, 22
Ch'ou, 6. See Comedian type
Comedian type, 6. See Ch'ou

Dance drama
    Ch'ang O's Flight to the Moon, 70
Dance numbers
    Ch'ang O's Flight to the Moon, 69, 70
    Dance in the Clouds, The, 44
    flag dance, the, 30
    Kuei-fei Intoxicated with Wine, 69
    pheasant plume dance, the, 30
    sleeve dance, the, 30
    streamer dance, the, 30
Drama, Chinese
    character types of, 81-83
        boxing master of, or *wu-ching*, 82
        ching (painted faces), 82

        ch'ing-i (good women), 40, 81
        ch'ou (comedian), 82
            played by T'ang Ming Huang, 83
        ch'ou-tan (*comédiennes*), 82
        "civil" (skilled in diction and singing), or *wên-shêng*, 81
        comedian, the, or *ch'ou*, 82
        comedians, military type, or *wu-ch'ou*, 82
        comédiennes, or *ch'ou-tan*, 82
        female impersonator, the, or *tan*, 81
        good women, or *ch'ing-i*, 81
        hsiao-shêng (youthful male), 81
        hua-tan (women of doubtful reputation), 81
        kuei-mên-tan (maidens), 81
        lao-shêng (old male), 81
        lao-tan (mothers or aged women), 81
        maidens, or *kuei-mên-tan*, 81
        male, the, or *shêng*, 81
        "military" (skilled in gymnastics), or *wu-shêng*, 81
        military woman, or *tao-ma-tan*, 81
        mothers or aged women, or *lao-tan*, 81
        old male, or *lao-shêng*, 81
        painted faces, or *ching*, 82
        shêng, or male, 81
        tan (or female impersonator), 81
        tao-ma-tan (military woman), 81
        wên-shêng (specialists in singing and diction), 81
        women of doubtful reputation, or *hua-tan*, 81
        wu-ching (specializes in bodily posture), 82
        wu-ch'ou (comedians, military type), 82
        wu-shêng (gymnasts; military performers), 81
        youthful male, or *hsiao-shêng*, 81
    characteristics of, 88-92
        announcer, or *fu mo chia mên*, 90

announcing one's name, or *t'ung ming*, 89
aside, the, or *pei kung*, 91
call, the, or *chiao pan*, 91
chiao pan (the call), 91
Chung-chou intonations, 89
couplets recited before going off the stage, or *hsia ch'ang tui lien*, 92
couplets when entering, or *shang chang tui chü*, 89
distinctive practices in, 88
flowery-faced one, or *hua-lien*, 92
fu mo chia mên (former announcer), 90
hsia ch'ang tui lien (couples recited before going off the stage), 92
hua-lien (flowery-faced one), 92
 walk of the, 93
intonations, the Chung-chou, 89
ko ch'ang (singing), 91
kuo mên (passing the door), 117
k'un-ch'ü employs lines of uneven length, 89
ku-tz'ŭ (recitations with the drum), 89
lines that actually open the play, or *ting ch'ang pai*, 89, 90
passing the door, or *kuo mên*, 117
pei kung (the aside), 91
poetry that opens the play, 89
poetry while sitting, or *tso shih*, 89
prologue, the, or *yin-tzŭ*, 88
recitations with the drum, or *ku-tz'ŭ*, 89
shang chang tui chü (couplets when entering), 89
similarity of, to French drama, 90
singing, or *ko ch'ang*, 91
singing, use of, to avoid monotony, 92
singing and declamation, 88
stage speech, marked by cadence and rhythm, 88
tien-chiang-ch'un tunes, 88
ting ch'ang pai (lines that actually open the play), 89, 90
tso shih (poetry while sitting), 89
t'ung ming (announcing one's name), 89
yin-tzŭ (prologue), 88
musical division of, 84-87
 Anhwei drama, pure, 86
  number of actors in company, 86
 Anhwei musical style, or *hui tiao*, 85
 beginnings of crude drama, 84
 ch'en (drama of Chenchung and Shensi), 85
 chen-ch'iang, 84
 Chenchung and Shensi drama, or *ch'en*, 85
 ching, 86
 ch'ou, 86
 costumes of Anhwei drama, 86
 êrh-huang, 87
  origin of, 85, 86
 female impersonators of Peking and Anhwei schools, 86
 hsi-p'i, origin of, 85
 hu-ch'in, use of, in *p'i-huang* music, 85, 86
  Yu-tien an artist on, 86
 i-yang (drama of Szechwan), 85
 Jade Hairpin, The, 85
 kao (drama of Kaoyang, Chihli), 85
 Kaoyang drama, or *kao*, 85
 k'un-ch'ü, the, 84
  associations for study of, 85
  " drama that Han itself had," 85
  place of, in Anhwei drama, 86
  reinstated by Mei Lan-fang, 85
 Kwangtung drama, or *yüeh-tiao*, 85
 lao-shêng, 86
 Music, Southern School of, 84
 Peking drama, a combination of the music of Hupeh and Anhwei, 85
 p'i-huang, 84, 87
  all-popular, 86
  combination of two styles, 86
  drama of Peking, 86
  lyrics of, set to *hu-ch'in*, 86
 shêng, 86
 Szechwan drama, or *i-yang*, 85
 Sporting by Dream in a Garden, 85
 tan, 86
 Three Pulls, 86
 yüeh-tiao (Kwangtung drama), 85
pantomime and acting, 93-96
 anger, 96
 dancing of Mei Lan-fang, 95
 dancing, the art of, 95
 departure from ancient custom in sleeping on stage, 95
 door, passing through a, 94
 entrance, 93
 exit, 93
 fighting, conventional stage, 95

INDEX

fingers, use of, by the *tan*, 94
hua-tan (when drinking tea), 94
modesty, 96
motioning a person away, 96
motioning a person to come, 96
movement in general, 94
passing through a door, 94
rice (eating), 95
running, 93
shêng, gait of the, 93
   when drinking tea, 94
sleeping, 95
sleeve, use of the, in tea drinking, 94
sleeves, use of, in weeping, 96
tan, short, mincing steps of the, 93
   use of the fingers by, 94
tea drinking, use of sleeve with, 94
taking wine and rice, 95
walking, 93
weeping, 96
wine (partaking of), 95
worry, 96
Sung dynasty, 89
Yüan dynasty, 89
Dream of the Red Chamber, The, 48

Encomium, an, translated from the Chinese, 66

Face painting
   origin of conventional, 82
Falsetto
   created to imitate a woman's voice, 18
   used by *hsiao-shêng*, 20
Female impersonator (see *tan*), 16
   definition of term, 16
   in Japan, 19
   on the Chinese stage, 17
   See onnagata, 19
Feng, Mr. K. K., speech of, 61
flute, the Chinese, 29. *See Hu-chin*
Friml, Mr. Rudolph, 57, 58

Galli-Curci, photographed and filmed with Chinese beauties, 57
Giles, Dr. Herbert A., 48

Head-dress of kingfisher feathers, 29
   use of, restored by Mei Lan-fang, 30
Heavenly Maiden Scattering Flowers, The, 29, 33, 66
   presented by Miss Kakuko Murata, 59

Hedges, Mr. Frank
   tribute of, 58
   warns against introducing foreign elements into Chinese theatrical art, 59
Hsiao-shêng, 20. *See* Rôle for youth
Hua-tan (vivacious woman), 40
   arts of the, 21, 22
   mischievous maidservant type, 42
   woman of questionable morals, 21
Hung Lou Mêng, 40
   tribute to, 48
Hu shü (beards and moustaches), 108, 109

Jade Hairpin, The (performed for the Crown Prince and Princess of Sweden), 56

King's Parting with His Favourite, The (performed for the Crown Prince and Princess of Sweden), 56
Kuei-men-tan, 20
   unmarried girl, 21, 22
Kuangho Lou, 6
   cradle, the, of theatrical profession, 7
   seating arrangement in, 6
K'un-ch'ü, 45
   sung to flute, 29

Lan-ling Wang, originator of conventional face painting, 82
Lao-tan, 20
   aged woman, 21, 22

Mei Chiao-ling, Mr., 87
Mei Lan-fang
   acting of, 68
   ancestral home of, 11
   birth of, 11
   characters impersonated by
     Chao Nü, 41, 42
     Chen Miao-ch'ang, 45
     Ch'un Hsiang, 43
     Heavenly Maiden, the, 44
     Hsi-jên, 49
     Tai-yü, 48, 49
     T'ien Nü, 43
     Tung-fang, 47
     Yang Kuei-fei, 42
   contributions of, to Chinese drama, 27
     ancient costume plays, 30
     combination of song and dance, 30
     dancing, revival of ancient, 95

INDEX

dramatic art school, 31
plays from the novel *Hung Lou Mêng*, 31, 32, 33
revival of ancient magnificent costumes, 30
dance as executed by, 69
début of, 11
declamation of, 68
dramatic criticism of, 65
dramas of
  Beauty in a Fisherman's Net, 35
  Betrothal at the Bright Tower, The, 67
  Ch'ang O's Flight to the Moon, 32
  Charming Hsi-jên, 49-51
  Fairy of the Guitar, The, 70
  Fateful Sword, The, 41
  Goddess of the River Lo, The, 35, 55
  Goddess Shang Yüan, The, 34
  Golden Mountain Monastery, 70
  Heavenly Maiden Scattering Flowers, The (dance drama), 33
  Hsi Shih, the Patriotic Beauty, 35
  Hung Hsien's Theft of the Box, 34
  Hung-i Kuan (Rainbow Pass), 46, 47
  Jade Hairpin, The (Yü Tsan Chi), 45
  King's Parting with His Favourite, The, 35
  Lovers, The Imprisoned, 32
  Love of Têng Hsia-ku, The, 31
  Ma Ku Offering Birthday Gifts, 34
  Mu-lan in the Army, 33
  Nun Seeks Love, A, 70
  Picking the Mulberry, 67
  Rainbow Pass (Hung-i Kuan), 46, 47, 70
  Red-Robed Empress, The, 70
  River Fan Pass, The, 70
  Smile, A Beauty's (Ching-wên Tearing the Fan), 33
  Strand of Flax, A, 32
  Tai-yü Burying the Blossoms, 32, 48, 49
  Three Pulls, 86
  Tien Nü San Hua, 43-45
  Washing the Yarn, 67
  Wild Goose Barrier, The, 68
  Yang Kuei-fei (T'ai Ch'ên Wai Chuan), 36
  Young Girl Kills a Serpent, A, 34
  Yü Chou Fêng (The Fateful Sword), 41, 42
  Yü Tsan Chi (The Jade Hairpin), 45, 46
emotional expression of, 68
face of, 67
foreign friends of
  Denby, Secretary of the U. S. Navy, 61
  Friml, Mr. Rudolph, 57
  Galli-Curci, 57
  Gustavus Adolphus, Crown Prince of Sweden, 56
  Hedges, Mr. Frank, 58
  Ichikawa, Mr. Sadanji, 60
  Louise Alexandra, Crown Princess of Sweden, 56
  Maugham, Mr. Somerset, 61
  Morita, Mr., 59, 60
  Murata, Miss Kakuko, 59
  Okura, Baron, 59
  Severn, Sir Claude, 56
  Shawn, Mr. Ted, 61
  St. Denis, Miss Ruth, 61
  Tagore, Dr. Rabindranath, 55
  Wood, General Leonard, 61
  Yamamori, Mr. S., 60
gifts to, 72, 73
grandfather of, 11
helped to revive older musical drama (see *k'un ch'ü*), 29
honoured by the ex-emperor Hsüan T'ung, 12
influence of name of, 5
in old dramas modernized, 70
interests of, 12
memoirs of, 11-13
merits of, a detailed catalogue of, 67-71
new musical scores created by, 69
postures in sword-horse rôles, 70
president Peking Actors' Association, 12
Shanghai visits of, 72
singing in *k'un-ch'ü* style, 70
sleeve, use of, by, 69
smile of, 68
social honours of, 73
stage death, as portrayed by, 69
stage walk of, 67
titles of
  "Foremost of the Pear Orchard," 12
  "Great King of Actors," 11, 86
theatrical idol of Chinese, 5

INDEX

tribute to, by Mr. Hsiu Mo, 67-71
vocal art of, 69
visit of, to Tokyo, 12
visit of, to leading cities of China, 71
waist of, 67
weeping of, 68
Military plays, or *Wu*, 70
Morita, Mr., 59
   response of, on behalf of Japanese actors, 60
Murata, Miss Kakuko, 59
Musical instruments, 117-121. See Chinese stage, musical instruments of the

Note, 2, 16
Novels, Chinese
   Dream of the Red Chamber, The, 48
   Hung Lou Mêng, 31, 40, 48, 49
   Three Kingdoms, The, 110

Operatic rôle, or *ch'ing-i*, 40

Pai, meaning of, 89
P'i-huang drama, 86, 87
   with *hu-ch'in*, 118. See Chinese violin
Plays mentioned
   Goddess Shang Yüan, The, 30
   Heavenly Maiden Scattering Flowers, The, 30
   Patriotic Beauty Hsi Shih, The, 30
   Yang Kuei-fei series, 30
Press notices
   Chinese newspaper account of visit of Mei Lan-fang to Hangchow, 71
   Mei News, 72
   North-China Daily News, 12, 13, 71

Quintet, a stringed
   Mei Blossom Suite, The, 57
   Willows Swaying Gold, 57
Quotations, 4
   China Journal (see page 20), 82

Seal, ancient, presented to Crown Prince and Princess of Sweden, 57
Shakespeare's England, extract from, 19
shêng, singing of, 92
Singing
   êrh-huang style, 69
   hsi-p'i style, 69
   k'un-ch'ü, intricate musical style, 70

Stage, the Chinese
   beards and moustaches, or *hu-hsü*, 108, 109
      beards, miscellaneous remarks on, 108, 109
      full beard, the, or *man jan*, 108
      hu hsü, colours of, 108
      man jan (full beard), 108
      san jan (tripart beard), 108
      short moustache, the, or *tuan jan*, 108
      tripart beard, the, or *san jan*, 108
      tuan jan (short moustache), 108
   costumes of the, 97-104
      ancient costume, or *ku chuang*, 103
      animal costumes, or *shou i*, 104
      arrow costume, the, or *chien i*, 102
      cape, the tasselled, or *yün chien*, 100
      chien i (arrow costume), 102
      ch'i i (Manchu coat), 101
      costumes for palace women, or *kung i*, 100
      ch'ün (the skirt), 99
         wearing of the, 99
      dragon robe, the, or *lung t'ao i*, 103
      eight-figured diagram robe, or *pa kua i*, 103
      eunuch's coat, the, or *t'ai chien i*, 99
      fighting costume, the, or *ta i*, 102
      fu kuei i (garment of wealth and distinction), 98
      glass abdomen, the, or *pien k'ao*, 103
      hsing-t'ou (wearing apparel), 97
      jacket and trousers, or *k'u ao*, 99
      jade belt, the, or *yü tai*, 99
      k'ai ch'ang (ordinary official robe), 101
         colour scheme and style of, 101
      k'ai k'ao (warrior's regalia), 101
         decorations of the, 101
         when worn with the *mang*, 101
      k'an chien (the vest), 99
      k'ao ch'i (military flags), 101
         colour schemes of, 101
         origin and use of, 101, 102
      kuan i (the official robe), 97
      k'u ao (jacket and trousers), 99
         as worn by the *hua-tan*, 99
      ku chuang (ancient costume), 103
         style reclaimed by Mei Lan-fang, 104
      kuei mên p'ei (maiden's gown), 98
      kung i (costumes for palace women), 100

INDEX

lao tou i (old person's garment), 98
lined coat, the, or *tieh-tzŭ*, 98
lung t'ao i (the dragon robe), 103
maiden's gown, or *kuei mên p'ei*, 98
ma kua (the riding jacket), 102
    black, embroidered with dragons, 103
    worn with the *ch'i i*, 101
Manchu coat, the, or *ch'i i*, 101
mang (robe), 97
military flags, or *k'ao ch'i*, 101
modern lined coat, or *shih shih tieh-tzŭ*, 100
official robe, or *k'ai ch'ang*, 101
pa kua i (eight-figured diagram robe), 103
    worn by Taoists, 103
p'ei (robe for banquets), 98
    colours and materials of, 98
pien k'ao (the glass abdomen), 103
    robe for female warriors, 103
riding jacket, the, or *ma kua*, 102
robe, the, or *mang*, 97
    for banquets, or *p'ei*, 98
    the official, or *kuan i*, 97
shang fu i (mourning weeds), 104
shih shih tieh-tzŭ (modern lined coat), 100
shou i (animal costumes), 104
shui (inner, or "water," sleeves), 97
skirt, the, or *ch'ün*, 99
sleeves, inner, or *shui*, 97
storm cloak, the, or *tou fêng*, 100
ta'i chien i (eunuch's coat), 99
ta i (fighting costume), 102
    description and use of, 102
tieh-tzŭ (lined coat), 98
    popular among female impersonators, 100
tou fêng (the storm cloak), 100
vest, the, or *k'an chien*, 99
warrior's regalia, or *k'ai k'ao*, 101
wearing apparel, or *hsing-t'ou*, 97
weeds of mourning, or *shang fu i*, 104
yün chien (the tasselled cape), 100
    worn over a *mang*, a *pei*, or a *kung i*, 100
yü tai, or jade belt, 99
    worn with a *mang* or a *kuan i*, 99
headgear and footwear, 105-107
    chih wei (pheasant plumes), 106
        by whom worn, 106

chin (soft hat), 106
fêng kuan (phœnix hat), 106
    by whom worn, 106
fêng mao (wind hat), 106
    description of, 106
fox-tails, or *hu wei*, 107
gauze hat, the, or *sha mao*, 105
helmet or hat, the, or *k'uei*, 105
hsüeh hsieh (shoes and boots), 107
hu wei (fox-tails), 107
k'uei (helmet or hat, the), 105
lo mao (military hat), 106
    style and decorations of, 106
military hat, the, or *lo mao*, 106
pheasant plumes, or *chih wei*, 106
phœnix hat, the, or *fêng kuan*, 106
sha mao (gauze hat), 105
    decorations of, 105
shoes and boots, or *hsüeh hsieh*, 107
soft hat, the, or *chin*, 106
wind hat, the, or *fêng mao*, 106
musical instruments of the, 117-121
    bell, the, or *p'êng chung*, 120
    ch'in, the, 45
    chiu yin lo (nine-toned gong), 121
    clarinet, the, or *so na*, 119
    cymbals, or *nao*, 120
    drum, the great, or *ta ku*, 118
    drum, the small, or *hsiao ku*, 117
    êrh-hu (two-stringed *hu*), 119
    flute, the, or *ti-tzŭ*, 45, 70, 119
    four-stringed *hu*, or *ssŭ-hu*, 119
    gong, the, or *lo*, 120
    gong, the small, or *hsiao lo*, 120
    hu-ch'in (so-called Chinese violin), 29, 44, 118
    lo (gong), 120
    hsiao ku (small drum), 117
    hsiao lo (small gong), 120
    hsien-tzŭ (three-stringed guitar), 118
    moon guitar, the, or *yüeh-chin*, 29, 118
    nao (cymbals), 120
    nine-toned gong, the, or *chiu yin lo*, 121
    pan (wooden time beater), 117
    pan-tzŭ, the, 88
    p'êng chung (bell), 120
    reed organ, the, or *shêng*, 45, 119
    shêng (reed organ), 45, 119
    so na (clarinet), 119
    ssŭ-hu (four-stringed *hu*), 119
    ta ku (great drum), 118

INDEX

three-stringed guitar, the, or *hsien-tzŭ*, 118
ti-tzŭ (flute), 119
ti-tzŭ, leading instrument in *kun-ch'ü* drama, 119
two-stringed *hu*, or *êrh-hu*, 119
violin, the Chinese, or *hu-ch'in*, 29, 44, 118
wooden time beater, the, or *pan*, 117
yin-tzŭ, 29
yüeh-ch'in (moon guitar), 29, 118
properties and symbolism, 110-116
    chair, the, or *i-tzŭ*, 113
        inside, or *nei chang i-tzŭ*, 113
        on its side, or *tao-i*, 113
        outside, or *wai chang i-tzŭ*, 113
    chang shan (long-handled fan), 114
    ch'ê ch'i (wagon flags), 110
        how manipulated, 111
    chiao-tzŭ (sedan), 111
    cho-tzŭ (table), 112
        objects represented by, 112, 113
    cloth city wall, or *pu ch'êng*, 111
    curtain, the great, or *ta chang-tzŭ*, 112
    duster, the, or *ying ch'ên*, 111
    fêng ch'i (wind flags), 112
    fu chieh (standard), 114
        use of the, 114
    flags on top of a soldier's spear, the, or *mên ch'iang ch'i*, 115
    horse-whip, the, or *ma pien*, 110
    hu (ivory tablet), 115
        when used, 115
    i-tzŭ (chair), 113
    ivory tablet, the, or *hu*, 115
    lantern, the, or *têng*, 114
    ling chien (mandate arrow), 113
        use of the, 113
    long-handled fan, the, or *chang shan*, 114
    mandate arrow, the, or *ling chien*, 113
    ma pien (horse-whip), 110
    mên ch'iang ch'i (flag on top of a soldier's spear), 115
        colours of, 115
    military weapons, or *ping ch'i*, 116
    miscellaneous small objects, made of wood, 115
    mountain rocks, or *shan shih p'ien*, 112
    ping ch'i (military weapons), 116
        made of wood, 116
    pu ch'êng (cloth city wall), 111
    sole bit of genuine scenery in Chinese drama, 111
    san (umbrella), 114
        oriental, how held, 114
    sedan, the, or *chiao-tzŭ*, 111
    shan shih p'ien (mountain rocks), 112
        symbolism of, 112
    shui ch'i (water flags), 112
    stage clouds, or *yün pien*, 115
    standard, the, or *fu chieh*, 114
    table, the, or *cho-tzŭ*, 112
    ta chang-tzŭ (great curtain), 112
        use of, 112
    tao-i (chair on its side), 113
    têng (lantern), 114, 115
    umbrella, the, or *san*, 114
    wagon flags, or *ch'ê ch'i*, 110
    wai chang i-tzŭ (chair outside), 113
        hair-splitting distinctions in regard to, 113
    water flags, or *shui ch'i*, 112
    wind flags, or *fêng ch'i*, 112
    wood, used in many small articles, 115
    ying ch'ên (duster), 111
        exalted position of, 111
    yün pien (stage clouds), 115
Sung dynasty, drama in, 89
Ssŭ-hsi Training School for Actors, 11

Tagore, Dr. Rabindranath, tribute of, 55, 56
Tan (definition of term), 16
    edict of emperor Ch'ien Lung, 17
    permanency of the. See Female impersonator, 16
    reason for the institution of the, 17
    singing of, 92
    six types of, on Chinese stage, 20
Ts'ai-tan, 20
    wicked woman, matchmaker, 21
    comic, lowly, detestable, 22
Theatre, the Chinese, 5
    closet method of study of, 4
    importance of the actor in the, 28
    social hall, a, 28
    to know their, is to know the Chinese people, 7
Three Kingdoms, The, 110
Training school, a, for male performers, 6, 87

Welcome, address of, to Japanese actors, 60

INDEX

Wu, the, or military plays, 70
Wu-tan, 20
    action of a, 47
    military maiden, 21

Yang Kuei-fei, impersonated by Mei Lan-fang, 19, 20
Yüan dynasty, drama in, 89
Yu-tien, uncle of Mei Lan-fang, artist on the *hu-ch'in*, 87